THE INTELLIGENT
RADICAL'S GUIDE
TO
ECONOMIC POLICY

Efficiency, Equality and the Ownership of Property
Planning and the Price Mechanism
The Geometry of International Trade
Problems of Economic Union
A Neo-Classical Theory of Economic Growth
Principles of Political Economy
The Stationary Economy
The Growing Economy
The Controlled Economy

The Control of Inflation (CUP)
Introduction to Economic Analysis and Policy (OUP)
Theory of International Economic Policy (OUP)

THE INTELLIGENT RADICAL'S GUIDE TO ECONOMIC POLICY

The Mixed Economy

by

James E. Meade

London   George Allen & Unwin Ltd
Ruskin House   Museum Street

HD
82
.M414
1975

Printed in Great Britain
in 10 point Baskerville type
by Clarke, Doble & Brendon Ltd
Plymouth

To M.M.

Preface

This short book may be regarded as a sequel to my *Planning and the Price Mechanism*, in which I tried in the immediate post-war atmosphere of 1947 to put down in simple language an economic philosophy for reconstruction and reform after the devastation of World War II. Much has happened since then and I have learned much, though my basic economic philosophy has remained unchanged. In the intervening years I have published a number of articles and delivered a number of lectures (listed in the Appendix on pages 155–56 below) written or spoken in plain English for the plain English man or woman, in which I have tried to develop this philosophy in the light of events and of my own education. The present state of economic turmoil and of unsettled ideas about the broad lines of economic policy makes it suitable, as it was in the years of post-war reconstruction, to reconsider the basic philosophy for our economic society.

In writing this book I have made use of many of the ideas expressed in the articles and lectures listed in the Appendix. From some of these I have incorporated some actual passages in the present text : in Chapter II from *The Control of Inflation* published by the Cambridge University Press, in Chapters II and III from *Prices and Wages in a Mixed Economy* published by the Institute of Economic Affairs, in Chapters V and VI from 'Poverty in the Welfare State' published in *Oxford Economic Papers*, in Chapter VII from 'Economic Policy and the Threat of Doom' published by the Academic Press in the Proceedings of the Ninth Annual Symposium of the Eugenics Society, and in Chapter IX from 'The Objectives of Economic Union' published by the Commission of the European Communities. To all these sources I would like to express my very grateful acknowledgements.

J. E. MEADE

Christ's College,
Cambridge.
August, 1974

Contents

I

The Objectives of Economic Policy

There are many social objectives which all reasonable citizens share in common : a decent standard of living, a decent distribution of income and wealth, individual liberty, individual security, individual participation in the making of decisions. Disagreement starts when these objectives conflict – when, for example, economic efficiency and a consequential high average standard of living is found to be dependent upon a less equal distribution of income and wealth than would otherwise be desirable. The radical in politics is the citizen who places a rather high relative value upon Liberty and Equality in the catalogue of social goods.

The intelligent radical does not ignore the other objectives of policy. He,[1] like others, will be much concerned with the encouragement of economic efficiency and with individual security and participation in decision-making. But above all he will dislike policies which lead to large concentrations of power which threaten personal independence, or to large concentrations of income and wealth which perpetuate class distinctions.

To achieve the radical's objectives a great shift of emphasis in present economic policies and institutions is needed in countries such as the United Kingdom.

A basic reform which the intelligent radical will support is the restoration and development of the free market mechanism where-ever it is possible to ensure workable competitive conditions. The great virtue of the competitive market mechanism is that it combines efficiency with freedom. Market rewards attract factors to produce at lowest possible cost what consumers most desire, but at the same time individuals remain free – without any extraneous compulsion by State, monopolistic employers, or restrictive labour unions – to purchase what they choose to purchase, to go where they choose to go, and to work at what they choose to work at.

The intelligent radical thus starts by advocating the removal

---

[1] By which, of course, I mean 'he or she'. Owing to the poverty of the English language in having no pronoun which covers both sexes I shall for brevity's sake write often in the masculine gender when it will, I hope, be clear from the context that I intend to cover both sexes equally.

of all unnecessary restrictions on the operation of free competitive markets. But he recognises that on the foundation of this market mechanism there must be built a superstructure of governmental interventions and controls. Some of these interventions are needed simply to set a background of conditions in which free competition can work effectively; others are needed to replace entirely the mechanism of competitive markets, where that mechanism cannot be expected to operate effectively; others have an intermediate purpose, namely to modify without replacing the operation of a market price mechanism.

Where social controls are necessary, the intelligent radical will advocate forms of intervention which interfere as little as possible with the continued operation of a free competitive market mechanism; and for this reason he will wish, wherever possible, to operate by means of taxes and subsidies and other rules determined on clear generalised, impersonal definitions and criteria rather than by *ad hoc* personal, bureaucratic, discretionary regulations.

We can enumerate the elements of the necessary superstructure of controls and interventions under the following eight headings.

First, the intelligent radical will be quick to realise that a free price mechanism must work in terms of money prices, money costs, money incomes, and the monetary values of capital and wealth. He will realise how impossible it becomes in such a monetary economy to avoid injustices and to make simple efficient decisions if the general level of money prices is rushing upwards or downwards at uncertain rates of inflation or deflation; he will realise how essential, therefore, it is to his purpose to control inflations and deflations and to do so by general financial means without resort to particular bureaucratic controls over particular prices, costs, and incomes. In present conditions it is, of course, the prospect of runaway inflation which is the major threat to the operation of a market mechanism.

Second, the intelligent radical will realise that the control of inflation requires not only governmental financial intervention through the budget and through monetary policy to stabilise the total level of money expenditures on goods and service; but, if unemployment and waste of resources is to be avoided, it requires also an appropriate response to market conditions on the part of money prices and costs, including wage rates. For this purpose, if for no other, governmental intervention is needed to submit to appropriate social controls the use of the monopolistic powers of large corporate concerns, whether these be huge conglomerate industrial concerns or powerful labour monopolies.

Third, in some cases economies of large scale are so important that monopoly is inevitable, as in the case of railway transport, the generation and distribution of electricity and such like services. In these cases the intelligent radical will advocate outright state ownership and control.

Fourth, there are many goods and services – such as the administration of justice and maintenance of law and order – which in the nature of things cannot be purchased separately by each individual for his own separate enjoyment, but which must be purchased and enjoyed in common by all members of the community. The intelligent radical will recognise the fact that in modern conditions the central and local governments must play a large role in the provision of such public goods.

Fifth, the intelligent radical is an egalitarian. He advocates State action to promote equality of opportunity. This involves such matters as the provision of equal access to educational opportunities and the prohibition of restrictive practices, such as restrictions by trade unions and professional associations which prevent a low-paid worker from improving his lot by entering into a higher-paid occupation. But equality of opportunity is not the same thing as equality of income and wealth. In a competitive system those citizens who are well endowed from birth with inborn capacity or inherited wealth and social contacts and who are favoured by the luck of the market may earn much higher incomes and accumulate much higher properties than the less fortunate members of society. The intelligent radical does not draw the conclusion that the competitive market should be abandoned, but rather that far-reaching direct fiscal measures should be taken by budgetary taxes and expenditures to moderate the high, and to supplement the low, incomes and properties.

Sixth, the intelligent radical realises that the market mechanism cannot be expected to deal adequately with planning for the uncertainties of the future, and that its operation may well be aided by some measure of governmental indicative planning.

Seventh, he also recognises the need for the central planning of large structural changes in the economy.

Finally, he recognises the need for controls and interventions in order to cope with important cases in which the market mechanism will otherwise neglect to take into account important items of social, as opposed to private, costs and benefits. Problems of environmental control, of the use of exhaustible resources, and of population growth will on these grounds be recognised as raising issues which call for governmental action.

This is indeed a formidable list of elements in the superstructure of governmental interventions to be constructed on the foundation of a freely operating market mechanism. Does it in fact leave any scope for economic freedom in a market mechanism?

It is impossible in fact always to make the best of both worlds; and there is, alas, often a clash between the freedom of an uncontrolled market and the need for some social control over particular individual actions. History presents a spectacle of fluctuating ideologies and fashions, mankind being drawn to put all the emphasis at one time on the virtues of the free market and at another time on the desirability of social controls. The intelligent radical keeps his head; he argues the virtues of the free market when the tendency is to think only of the need for particular interventions and he stresses the need for social interventions whenever *laissez-faire* becomes an object of religious devotion.

At the present time the swing of opinion from the nineteenth-century doctrines of *laissez-faire* has gone so far as to obscure the advantages of a free market mechanism; and for this reason the intelligent radical for the moment puts special emphasis on reforms of a kind which will restore the efficient operation of that mechanism wherever it can be effectively restored. This restoration is the subject matter of Chapters II, III, and IV of this book. The subsequent Chapters are then devoted to the superstructure of controls and interventions which must be built upon this foundation.

The combinations of freedom and control advocated in this short book carry with them at least some far-reaching implications; and the set of policies which they involve will never be capable of implementation unless there is some measure of consensus of opinion as to their desirability. At least three major changes of attitude are needed.

First, the emphasis which the intelligent radical places on individual freedom and equality involves encouraging small-scale rather than large-scale types of enterprise. This may involve some sacrifice of technical progress and of growth of the kind which insists on the output of a larger and larger supply of high-technology products. Independence, leisure, and a more equitable distribution of the real goods of life need to be valued more highly relatively to a greater and greater affluence in command over more and more sophisticated industrial products.

Second, the intelligent radical will never persuade his fellow citizens to let the market mechanism freely play its part, unless the ugly face of capitalism is beautified. Institutions and attitudes need to be changed in a way which makes it impossible for huge riches to be amassed by obscure financial fiddles, tax avoidance, and speculation on rapidly inflating values.

Third, the decent, free, prosperous society which modern science has undoubtedly brought within our grasp can never be achieved if powerful monopolistic bodies are unwilling to accept social controls over their actions.

This doctrine must be accepted by powerful labour unions as well as by large industrial concerns; but this cannot be done in the absence of a widespread change of public opinion. We should at least have learned by now that, while suitable legislation may be necessary for the social control of labour monopolies, such legislative provision cannot be made effective unless there is a consensus of public opinion in favour of their enforcement.

But trade unionists and their leaders are reasonable men and women. They will surely themselves come to recognise that an economy cannot be properly run in conditions in which each of a number of independent monopolies, each alone capable of bringing the economy to a standstill, insists on preserving its separate independence of action in enforcing its own separate demands upon the community. There is no hope for a decent free society unless there grows up some widespread acceptance of the view, first, that all powerful monopolies — including labour monopolies — should be subject to appropriate social controls and, second, that it is for parliament to decide what that form of control should be. With universal free suffrage the mass of the electorate can then decide whether it wishes the form of control to be modified.

We are a long way from this state of affairs at the moment; but the intelligent radical does not despair. History suggests that ideologies, given time, can be basically revised by persistent education and persuasion; and he may sense that among the young there are already signs of a growing impatience with large concentrations of wealth and with large centralised organisations of power and privilege. He will peg away using reasonable arguments to persuade reasonable citizens to accept reasonable policies.

B

II

The Control of Inflation

A necessary condition for the design of an effective set of radical economic policies and institutions is the existence of a monetary unit of account with a more or less dependable, stable, real purchasing power. Accordingly in this chapter we shall attempt to outline : first, the mechanisms of price inflation; second, the disadvantages, particularly for the radical's set of policies, of price inflation; and, third, in the light of the mechanisms and disadvantages of inflation the design of policies for the control of inflation by means which will help rather than hinder the intelligent radical's package of other economic policies.

By inflation we mean simply a rise in the general level of money prices of goods and services. The causes of an inflationary situation are often divided into two groups, namely those which originate from a demand inflation and those which originate from a cost inflation. It is convenient to consider the phenomenon of price inflation under these two broad headings, though, as we shall see, the two types of inflation are in fact very closely interconnected.

A demand inflation occurs when there is 'too much money chasing too few goods'. The total demand for the goods and services produced in a country can be catalogued under the following four heads : (1) the expenditure by individual citizens for the purchase of domestically produced goods and services for individual consumption – food, clothing, heating, and other consumption goods; (2) the expenditure by business concerns on domestically produced buildings, machinery, plant, and other equipment in order to invest in additional productive capacity; (3) the purchase by the government and local authorities of domestically produced goods and services for public purposes; and (4) the purchase by foreigners of exports of the country's domestically produced goods and services.

In a dynamic world all of these elements of total national expenditure will be jolted from time to time by technological, political, or other shocks. Thus, to take one or two special examples, a change in the level of economic activity in the rest of the world – e.g. an American boom or slump – may cause foreigners to demand more or less of the country's exports. Or, a change in businessmen's expectations of profit – e.g. caused by an important technological invention – may lead to a rise or a fall in the demand for new capital equipment. Or a political event may lead to an important change in the level of governmental expenditures – e.g. a rearmament programme or a reduced expenditure on arms resulting from an international disarmament agreement.

It is not intended in this short book to discuss the ways in which these various elements of total national money expenditure may react upon each other. Any such discussion would involve far-reaching technical economic analysis. It must suffice to point out that variations of the kind enumerated in the previous paragraph can lead to large fluctuations in the total national demand for goods and services. These fluctuations are in fact partially cumulative since a rise in the demand for new machinery, for example, will tend to raise the money incomes of the producers of machines who will then have more to spend on consumption goods of various kinds. In consequence those who produce these particular consumption goods will not only receive higher incomes to spend on other consumption goods, but may also be induced to spend capital funds on new plant and equipment to meet the larger demand for their products. And so on in a series of waves of expansion of demand.

But in addition to these spontaneous, exogenous fluctuations in expenditures of various kinds, the financial authorities themselves can take action to affect the level of total money expenditures.

These financial controls can be enumerated under four heads : (1) the government can increase its own budgetary expenditures on goods and services; (2) the government by lowering rates of taxation can leave a larger sum of freely disposable income in the hands of private individuals and thus induce a rise in their demand for consumption goods; (3) the banking authorities can lower the rates of interest or otherwise ease the terms on which they will lend new funds and can thus encourage the borrowing of new funds for expenditure on investment in new capital equipment; and (4) the rate of exchange between the pound and foreign currencies can be depreciated, thus making domestically produced goods cheaper relatively to foreign produced goods and thus in due course encouraging foreigners to purchase more exports from this country and domestic purchasers to purchase less imports and more home-produced goods.

By any combination of these four types of financial policy

the authorities can raise the total level of money expenditures on domestically produced goods and services; and by any combination of the corresponding opposite policies they can damp down the total level of money expenditures.

Let us see what happens if the total level of money expenditures is being increased, either because of spontaneous changes in the demands of private citizens or because of governmental financial policies. If we start from a position of economic depression with heavy unemployment of labour and underutilisation of capital equipment, the effects of the increased demand may be to induce a greater output of goods to be sold at uninflated prices. But if we start from a position of full employment with capital equipment used up to capacity, the increased demand for goods and services can lead only to a rise in the prices at which the existing level of output will be sold.

If this were the whole story, the avoidance of inflation would in principle be a relatively simple matter. Let the authorities use their financial controls to maintain total demand at a level which will provide a market at uninflated prices for the whole output which the national economy will produce at full employment; but let them damp down the total level of money expenditures whenever the expansion of expenditures tends to lead to price increases rather than to increases in output. But, alas, this is to neglect the second element in the causation of inflation, namely the element of cost inflation.

Suppose that there is full employment of labour and that in this situation, as a result of investment in a new capital equipment and the advance of technological knowledge, output per head in industry in general is rising at a rate of 2 per cent per annum. Suppose, however, that the labour unions are in general demanding successfully a rate of rise of wage earnings of 5 per cent per annum. As a result wage cost per unit of output will be rising by approximately 3 per cent per annum. Suppose that the financial authorities so control the general level of money expenditure as to prevent any rise in the selling prices at which producers can sell their produce. The inevitable result will be a reduction in output and a growth of unemployment. For a short time the 3 per cent per annum rise in wage costs may simply eat into profit margins. But this cannot continue for long. Sooner or later profits would be reduced to zero and then turned into losses. Indeed it is impossible for the workers as a whole for long to obtain a 5 per cent per annum increase in real wages when output per head is increasing only at 2 per cent per annum.

The financial authorities are now faced with a dilemma : *either* to control total demand so as to prevent a rise in the selling prices of output and to see unemployment grow *or else* to allow total money expenditures to be expanded at a rate which will permit selling prices to be raised by 3 per cent per annum so that wage costs and selling prices keep in line with each other. If there is a political commitment to full employment, they must choose the latter course.

An inflationary rise of prices at 3 per cent per annum may seem a small price to pay for full employment; and indeed it would be a small price to pay. But that, alas, is not the end of the story if the labour unions, when they insisted on a wage rise of 5 per cent per annum, had in mind a rise in real wages, not merely in money wages, of 5 per cent per annum. In that case when the selling prices of output, i.e. the cost of living, is found to be rising at 3 per cent per annum, they will demand a rate of rise of wages of 8 per cent per annum – 3 per cent to offset the rising cost of living and 5 per cent to give a real increase in purchasing power. But with wage rates rising by 8 per cent per annum and productivity rising only by 2 per cent per annum wage costs will be rising by 6 per cent per annum. If then to preserve full employment, selling prices and the cost of living are allowed to rise by 6 per cent per annum, a real rise of wages of 5 per cent will be achieved only by a rise of money wages of 11 per cent (6 plus 5 per cent). This in turn means that wage costs rise by 9 per cent (11 per cent minus 2 per cent productivity increase), which requires a 9 per cent rise in prices to ensure full employment. And so on, in an unending cumulative explosion, until there is an infinitely rapid rate of inflation of money prices and wages.[1]

---

[1] There is another phenomenon in wage fixing which may lead to an explosive inflation by a similar, though not identical, process. Suppose that one set of workers (group A) consider that they ought to be paid 10 per cent more than another (group B), but that group B consider that they should be paid at least as much as group A. Start with the same wage rate for both groups. Group A then demands a rise of 10 per cent to restore a 10 per cent differential over group B. Group B then demands a rise of 10 per cent to restore equality. Group A then demands a second 10 per cent to restore the differential, followed by group B demanding a further 10 per cent to remove the differential. And so on. The leap-frogging of group A over group B and of group B over group A will lead to an unending rapid rate of inflation. The cost inflation may become more and more rapid if groups A and B, as they learn what is happening, react more and more quickly in their attempts to outpace each other in the restoration of their incompatible differentials.

A major disadvantage of inflation, even if it can be prevented from becoming explosive, is that it causes inequitable redistributions of income and property so long as some forms of income and property remain fixed in money terms. So long as social payments such as old-age pensions and family allowances remain fixed in terms of money, a continuing inflation causes them to receive less in real terms than is planned for them. Persons who have invested their savings in various forms of money deposits or in life insurance policies fixed in money terms lose relatively to those whose property is invested in land or other real assets, the prices of which may be expected to be inflated in line with the general level of commodity prices. In many cases it is the poor who lose and the rich who gain from inflation. In any case the redistribution is haphazard and unplanned.

It may be argued that an easier, and to that extent more desirable, way of dealing with this aspect of inflation is to take measures to insure the recipients of fixed or sluggish money incomes against the evils of price inflation rather than to put a stop to the inflation itself. Thus, as is increasingly happening in this country, not only money wage rates, but also old-age pensions and other social benefits can be tied to the cost-of-living index or to an index of the rise of other money incomes in the community, in order to guarantee the recipients of such incomes against the ravages of future price inflation. On grounds of social justice there is everything to be said for such arrangements; it is right and proper that such people should receive the real share of the national income which is planned for them. But such measures are no substitute for the control of inflation itself; indeed they make it even more likely that radical anti-inflationary measures must be taken if an explosive inflation and a collapse of the currency is to be avoided.

Fundamentally, an explosive inflationary pressure is generated when the slices which various independent competing groups of citizens attempt to take out of the national cake together add up to more than the whole cake. We have already illustrated this in our parable in which all workers attempt to increase their real incomes by 5 per cent per annum though output per worker is increasing only by 2 per cent per annum. In such a case the citizens' efforts to increase their real incomes through large increases in their money incomes will be frustrated by an unexpectedly rapid inflation of the cost of living. But so long as there are some citizens who are not making excessive claims and whose incomes are fixed or sluggish in terms of money, the frustration of those who are making excessive claims will be less complete and less immediate. They can make real gains at the expense of those whose money incomes are not rising so fast. But the experience of a quickening rate of inflation causes more and more wage rates and more and more other incomes, such as old-age pensions, to be tied *de facto* or *de jure* to the cost of living; and in so far as those whose incomes were previously sluggish or fixed in terms of money now join in the game and insist that their incomes too be raised quickly in response to price rises, the rate of increase in money costs and money prices will accelerate.

We all start with a certain money illusion. We think of our income in terms of money and we have ideas in our head as to what is the proper sort of price to pay for this or that service or product. A reasonably efficient monetary system for financing transactions and for recording commercial values is of inestimable importance in any modern society and in particular in the kind of liberal market economy which the intelligent radical will favour. The existence of a straightforward, simple monetary accounting system rests upon our continuing to think in terms of money. Measures which tie money incomes, money debts, and other money payments to the cost of living encourage the abandonment of this most desirable habit of thinking in terms of money. The more people concentrate their thoughts not on their money incomes, debts, and payments but upon the real value of their money incomes, debts, and payments, the more rapidly will they try to get rid of their money when they expect prices to rise; and this flight from money into goods will itself accelerate the rate of price inflation. The ultimate result can well be a complete distrust of the currency and the disastrous disorganisation of business and economic life which would ensue when there was no readily acceptable monetary counter for transactions. Complete currency collapses are not unknown to the historian and there is no reason to believe that 'it cannot happen here'.

But with a rapid and possibly explosive rate of price inflation many serious inequities, inefficiencies, and inconveniences arise long before a currency actually collapses. A few examples must suffice.

The mortgage problem is an outstanding example. Suppose that in the absence of any price inflation the rate of interest would be 5 per cent per annum, because this represents the real rate of return which people can earn in the market on real capital savings and investment. At 5 per cent per annum a capital sum of £10,000 will provide an annuity of £802 for twenty years.

Apply this to the mortgage market. A newly married couple who wanted to raise £10,000 to purchase a house would have to pay £802 a year for twenty years to repay the principal with interest at 5 per cent per annum.

Suppose now that the real underlying conditions remain unchanged but that a general price inflation of 10 per cent per annum is taking place and is expected by all lenders and borrowers to continue for the next 20 years. The rate of interest on a money loan must rise from 5 to $15\frac{1}{2}$ per cent per annum in order to give the same yield in real terms.[1] But at a rate of interest of $15\frac{1}{2}$ per cent per annum the borrower must make twenty annual payments of no less than £1,642 in order to meet the interest and repay the principal on a loan of £10,000. The newly married couple this year out of the same initial income must face an annual mortgage payment for twenty years of £1,642 instead of only £802 simply because there is now a prospect of a 10 per cent per annum rate of price inflation in the future. They may find it impossible to do so out of their current income.

Where is the snag? Why do they appear to be so badly hit although the lender of the £10,000 is only to receive the same real rate of return of 5 per cent per annum? The answer is simple. The newly married couple by paying a fixed annuity of £1,642 instead of £802 will in the early years of the payment be bearing a much heavier mortgage burden (twice as heavy in the first year); but as time passes with prices rising by 10 per cent per annum this annual payment will become less and less valuable in real terms. If the newly married couple's money income rises with the inflation by 10 per cent per annum, then by the end of twenty years it will be 6·73 times as large as it would have been in the absence of inflation. In real values the annuity £1,642 will have fallen by the twentieth year to £244. In other words by the twentieth year the borrower's annual payment of £1,642 will be worth only £244 in terms of its initial real purchasing power, whereas in the absence of inflation he would still be making an annual payment worth £802 in constant real purchasing power.

Thus the newly married couple in times of inflation have to pay very heavily in real terms in the early years of the annual mortgage payment (at a rate, indeed, which may be beyond the reach of their current income), but have a very much reduced

---

[1] If someone invests £100 at $15\frac{1}{2}$ per cent, he will have £115·5 at the end of the year. If prices have then risen by 10 per cent from £1 to £1·1, he will be able to buy 115·5/1·1 = 105 units of goods at the end of the year.

real burden to face in the later years of their mortgage payment. The problem could be met if institutional arrangements were set up for the tying of loans to a price index. If our newly married couple had been able to borrow £10,000 for twenty annual payments which would themselves rise by 10 per cent per annum (in line with the rise in the general level of prices), then their annual payments would once more start at £802 in the first year, rising by 10 per cent each year till they reached £5,397 in the twentieth year. In this case the real burden on the borrower would once more remain constant.

Institutional developments in the capital market which would make provision for lenders and borrowers to tie their obligations to a cost-of-living or other price index could thus provide a proper solution to the mortgage problem in times of inflation, though it is only one more example of the abandonment of calculation in terms of money and one more step towards the ultimate abandonment of the currency. In the absence of any such indexing arrangement there is likely to be strong political pressure put upon the government to keep down the rate of interest on mortgages in order to reduce the initial burden on our newly married couple. For example, at a rate of interest of 10 per cent the annual payment over twenty years to repay capital with interest on a £10,000 loan would be £1,175 (i.e. intermediate between the £802 at an interest rate of 5 per cent and the £1,642 at an interest rate of 15½ per cent per annum).

This solution is highly inequitable and fraught with further inflationary danger.

If prices are rising at 10 per cent a year, then the lender of money at 10 per cent per annum is obtaining no real return on his money. The lender will in fact be lending to the borrower at a zero real rate of interest. Whereas in the absence of inflation the lender would have obtained, and our newly married couple would have paid, a real rate of interest of 5 per cent a year, now with inflation the newly married couple is receiving its loan at a zero real rate of interest. In fact the annual payment of £1,175 is sufficient merely to repay the real value of the loan. This highlights the paradox of the effect of inflation on the mortgage market; the newly married couple will feel hardly treated because they have to pay, out of the same present income, £1,175 a year instead of £802 a year on their borrowing, while in fact the inflation is, over the period of the loan, subsidising them at the expense of the lender. The paradox is solved when one realises that the newly married couple is being subsidised in real terms over the twenty years of the loan, but is having to pay rather more in real terms during the early years and a great deal less in real terms in the later years.

But this solution is not only unfair to the lender (who may well be a small saver lending his limited funds through a building society); it is extremely dangerous in that it will stoke up the inflation. To bring interest rates down from 15½ per cent to 10 per cent when prices are expected to rise by 10 per cent means that the monetary authorities must be prepared to pump new money into the capital market, since borrowers of all kinds can expect to make 15½ per cent on many forms of investment (i.e. 10 per cent rise in the money value of the capital goods plus a 5 per cent real rate of return on the capital equipment). Excessive borrowing for capital expenditures will result and the increased level of the total national demand for goods and services will stoke up the rate of demand inflation.

The unhappy plight of the lender of money loans in times of price inflation is still further intensified by taxation. Income tax is designed to be a tax on real income. But consider once more the saver who lends his money at 15½ per cent when prices are rising at 10 per cent. If the real return on capital is 5 per cent, in the absence of taxation the lender does not lose. He obtains a real rate of return of 5 per cent on his loan, the higher money interest rate (15½ per cent instead of 5 per cent) making up for the 10 per cent fall in the value of his money loan. But this is not so if there is an income tax on his interest. Suppose that the rate of income tax were 33⅓ pence in the pound. Then in the absence of inflation with a 5 per cent rate of interest on a loan of £100 a lender would receive a gross interest of £5 which after tax would give him £3·33 or a net real rate of return of 3⅓ per cent. This is presumably the real effect which a tax of 33⅓ per cent is intended to have. But suppose now that prices rise at 10 per cent a year and that the rate of interest rises to 15½ per cent to make up for the inflation. The lender receives a gross interest income of £15½ a year which after tax leaves a net interest income of £10⅓. As prices are rising at 10 per cent, he can maintain the real value of his capital intact only by adding virtually the whole of his net post-tax interest income to his savings. The real return on his savings has been reduced to zero, because what was designed as a tax on real income has become now also a tax on real capital.[1]

[1] If our lender is lending at only 10 per cent when prices are rising at 10 per cent (because the monetary authorities are keeping down the

But direct lending and borrowing in terms of money is not the only kind of transaction which raises monetary accounting problems of the kind which we have examined at some length in the case of the mortgage market. Consider the problem of depreciation allowances. Consider a machine costing £10,000 which is expected to have a useful life of 20 years. In the absence of price inflation, if the machine is to be replaced at the end of its life, the business must have deducted from its profits year by year an amount which will have accumulated to £10,000 by the end of the twenty years. One method is by a straight-line depreciation, i.e. by putting aside each year from the concern's total gross income of profits, interest etc. one-tenth of the value of the machine, so that, in our example, £500 a year for twenty years will amount to £10,000 for the purchase of the new machine.

Suppose now that prices are rising by 10 per cent per annum. Then a machine which cost initially £10,000 will cost no less than £67,300 in twenty years time. If the concern puts aside each year only one-twentieth of the original cost of the machine, it will have only £10,000 towards the £67,300 needed for the replacement of the machine. If it wishes to put aside a constant sum each year, it must put aside £3,365 a year instead of £500 a year for depreciation. Otherwise it will have treated as real net profit over the ten years some sums which were in fact needed to keep its real capital intact.[1]

The implications of this discrepancy for tax purposes are hair-raising. Accounts for tax purposes must be kept in monetary terms as if money values were stable. A business will be allowed to deduct from its gross profits only enough in depreciation allowances to replace the money value, not the real quantity, of its original capital. In the above example it will be able to deduct

money rate of interest), then on a loan of £100 he will receive a gross interest income of £10 a year which, after tax at 33⅓ per cent, leaves £6⅔ a year. His £100 will have accumulated only to £106⅔, but the price level will have risen from £1 to £1·1. In real terms the value of his capital has *fallen* from 100 to 106·6/1·1 = 96, so that he will be earning a real rate of interest of *minus* 4 per cent per annum. The tax which was designed to take away one-third of his real income has taken away the whole of his real income plus 4 per cent of his real capital wealth.

[1] It is insufficient merely to start with an annual depreciation allowance of £500 and to raise this by 10 per cent per annum to keep in line with the inflation of prices. This policy would result in a total depreciation fund at the end of twenty years of only £31,515 to meet the replacement cost of £67,300. Each year's money depreciation allowance must be geared not merely to the then current cost of a new machine but to what the machine will cost in the future year when it will need to be replaced.

£500 a year and not £3,365 a year as a cost against its gross profits.

The taxation implications of such a system of book-keeping in monetary terms in inflationary conditions can be illustrated in its most dramatic form by considering the replacement of a stock of raw materials rather than the depreciation and replacement of a durable machine. Consider the example of a business which in the absence of inflation consists in the purchase of £100,000 worth of materials at the beginning of the year, the expenditure of £5,000 in wages on these materials during the year, and the sale of these materials for £110,000 at the end of the year. The business will show a gross profit of £5,000 after replacement of the stock of materials, of which we suppose 50 per cent to be paid in tax leaving a post-tax profit of £2,500. This simple account may be expressed as follows :

(1) *Non-Inflationary Account*

Receipts	£	*Expenses*	£
Sale of worked up		Wages	5,000
materials	110,000	Replacement of	
		materials	100,000
		Profit	5,000
	£110,000		£110,000

Suppose now that all the underlying real quantities remain the same but that all prices rise by 10 per cent in the course of the year. The business will sell its output for £121,000 instead of £110,000. Its wage bill will be £5,500 instead of £5,000. The cost of replacement of its materials will be £110,000 instead of £100,000. If one allowed the cost of replacement of the same real stock of materials as a business expense, profits would also have gone up by 10 per cent. The account would be as follows :

(2) *Real Accounting in Inflationary Conditions*

Receipts	£	*Expenses*	£
Sale of worked up		Wages	5,500
materials	121,000	Replacement of	
		materials	110,000
		Profit	5,500
	£121,000		£121,000

But this is not how accounts must be kept in monetary terms for tax purposes. For tax purposes one is allowed to count as an expense only the cost of replacement of capital to the same monetary value as its original value. The account for tax purposes will be :

(3) *Monetary Accounting in Inflationary Conditions*

Receipts	£	Expenses	£
Sale of worked up		Wages	5,500
materials	121,000	Replacement of	
		stock to	
		original value	100,000
		Profit	15,500
	£121,000		£121,000

If the rate of tax on profit is 50 per cent, this business will now be charged £7,750 in tax leaving a net post-tax 'profit' of £7,750. But if the business wishes to remain in business on the same scale as before it must find £110,000 instead of the £100,000 for the replacement of its stock. Its account will then be :

(4) *Real Replacement with Monetary Accounting in Inflationary Conditions*

Receipts	£	Expenses	£
Sale of worked up		Wages	5,500
materials	121,000	Replacement of	
		original real	
		stock	110,000
		Tax on 'profit'	7,750
		Post-tax loss	−2,250
	£121,000		£121,000

The firm has no net profit left to pay a dividend or to invest in a real expansion of its business. Indeed it is £2,250 out of pocket if it merely maintains the existing scale of its operations; it must borrow merely in order to stay in business. Such a situation is clearly fraught with danger. The firm will be reported as having made a pre-tax profit of £15,500 as a result of the inflation – more than three times as large as the non-inflationary profit of £5,000. Yet in fact it is making a loss and being driven out of business. The understandable political cry will be : 'Raise the tax on these profiteers from inflation.' The result will be the collapse of free enterprise – much to the delight of the authoritarians and much to the sorrow of the intelligent radical.

The problems of mortgage finance and of depreciation

allowances have been chosen merely as particular illustrations of the inequities and inefficiencies which are introduced into the economy because of the complexities of accounting in terms of money in conditions of rapid price inflation. Many other examples could be given, since any accounting (whether by individuals, by businesses, or by government) which involves comparing values at one time with values at another time will raise these complexities. These disadvantages of inflation are real enough; but the intelligent radical will realise that there is a further underlying and much more serious threat to the sort of society which he favours.

This threat arises from the fact that as the rate of inflation explodes and the need to contain it becomes more and more urgent, control measures may well be adopted which are in direct conflict with the sort of policy arrangements which the radical advocates for the attainment of other social objectives. In particular there may well be attempts to keep down money prices and costs by a whole range of controls over particular goods and services with a consequential impairment of the competitive market mechanism, with a vast extension of bureaucratic discretionary controls, and with great particular inequities. Let us give a few examples.

Certain prices, such as the rents of private dwellings, may be frozen. As a result the real rent received by the landlord and the real rent payable by the tenant falls progressively as other money prices and incomes rise. This is grossly inequitable as between the landlord (who is not always rich) and the tenant (who is not always poor). It is grossly inefficient in that it removes all private incentive to construct dwellings to let or to maintain present dwellings in good repair. This in turn makes it more and more necessary for the authorities to regulate the behaviour of landlords and tenants and themselves to become the sole providers of rented dwellings.

If the rate of inflation is sufficiently threatening, attempts may be made not merely to control one or two particular prices, but to adopt a prices-and-incomes policy which involves controlling the whole range of prices, wage rates, and other incomes. Assume for the moment that this is politically possible. It is inconceivable that bureaucratic regulations could be devised which over any considerable period would keep the myriads of prices, costs, and incomes at a stable average level but with sufficient relative flexibility to preserve both efficiency and equity as conditions changed in various sectors of a modern complex economy. The loss in the long run of the freedoms and efficiencies of a competitive market system would be enormous.

To take an example of a different kind, suppose that (in the way which we have already examined), in order to moderate the mortgage charges for new borrowers for the purchase of houses, interest rates are kept at or below the expected rate of inflation. As we have seen, borrowers can then borrow at a zero or negative real rate of interest. Particular measures may then be required to prevent this from stoking up the inflationary pressure through the borrowing of these exceptionally cheap funds for excessive expenditures on capital development. But if loans for mortgages are to be kept at 10 per cent, while other borrowers are to behave as if the rate had been raised to $15\frac{1}{2}$ per cent, a whole battery of particular interventions will be necessary. Borrowers for other purposes must by one form of bureaucratic regulation or another be prevented from having access, directly or indirectly through the growth of black markets, to the cheap funds which are designed for mortgages on new houses.[1]

If we are to achieve the sort of society which would delight the

---

[1] One method for preventing an unduly low money rate of interest from leading to excessive borrowing is to disallow the borrower from deducting his loan interest from his other income for tax purposes. This may in the circumstances be better than nothing; but it is inequitable and inefficient as compared with raising the rate of interest to its proper level and then allowing deduction of debt interest. Suppose that in the absence of inflation the rate of interest were 5 per cent; that a trader invests £100 of borrowed money in a stock of goods; and that in the outcome he just breaks even making a trading profit of £5 which just covers his interest payment of £5. In real terms this is an investment which just covers its costs. With a 50 per cent rate of income tax the proper arrangement would be that the lender should pay a tax of £2½ on his receipt of £5 of interest and that the borrower, whose net profit after interest was deducted was zero, should pay no tax. This again leaves the borrower with just the correct investment incentive, namely to seek any investment which would do better than this and to avoid any investment which would do worse. Suppose now that in the same real situation prices are rising by 10 per cent, but that the money rate of interest is held down to 10 per cent. The borrower of £100 now makes a gross profit of some £15 (i.e. his real trading profit of £5 plus £10 appreciation due to the rise in price of his stock). If he is allowed to deduct the interest payment of £10 from his gross profit of £15, he pays £2·5 in tax and £10 in interest, leaving a net profit of £2·5. If he is not allowed to deduct the interest payment, he pays £10 in interest plus £7·5 in tax on his gross profit of £15, leaving him with a net loss of £2·5. To allow deduction of interest for the calculation of tax has made this marginal investment unnaturally profitable; but to disallow deduction of interest has made it unnaturally unprofitable.

heart of the intelligent radical, there is only one possible form of
inflation control. The financial authorities must, through their
monetary and budgetary policies, so stabilise the total level of
expenditures throughout the economy as to prevent an uncontrolled inflation of monetary values. But at the same time, in
order to prevent this from leading to heavy unemployment, conditions must be restored in free markets to ensure that money
prices and costs (including wage rates) are not pushed up beyond
the levels which allow all resources to find full, profitable employment at this stabilised level of monetary demand for goods and
services.

This raises three questions. First, what sort of criterion should
be adopted for the stabilisation of total money expenditures?
Second, can the authorities exert the necessary influences over
total money expenditures? Third, in what way can prices and costs
(including wage rates) be made sufficiently responsive to market
conditions to prevent serious unemployment? We conclude this
chapter with a brief discussion of the first two of these questions.
The crucial question is the third, and will form the subject matter
of the two following chapters.

What then should be the nature of any criterion which might
be chosen for stabilisation? The essential requirement is simply
that there should exist some reliable rule about monetary developments which possesses two qualities : first, it should be simple
and easy to understand so that people can plan their monetary
assets and obligations with a confident understanding about future
monetary conditions and, second, it should be such as to rule out
immoderate rates of inflation or deflation of the general level of
prices.

One obvious criterion which fulfils these conditions is so to
control money expenditures on goods and services as to maintain
a completely stable level of selling prices.[1] An alternative possibility is so to control money expenditures on goods and services
as to maintain a steady, but moderate, predetermined rate of
growth of the total of money incomes.

Let us consider first the nature of the price index which might
be chosen for stabilisation if the first of these two criteria were
to be applied.

It would be unwise to choose the ordinary cost-of-living index
which is much influenced both by the price of imports and by the

---

[1] Or more accurately expressed : 'to maintain the highest possible level
of economic activity which is compatible with a general price index not
rising above a predetermined ceiling level'.

level of indirect taxes. Suppose that the cost-of-living index were chosen and that the terms of international trade were then to turn against this country because the price of imports (such as oil) had risen. A decline in the real income of the citizens of this country below what it would otherwise have been would be inevitable for reasons outside the control of this country's authorities. But in order to stabilise the cost-of-living index when the import content of the index had risen, the authorities would have to take disinflationary measures to drive down the price of home-produced goods in order to offset the rise in the price of imported goods. But unless money wage costs could be quickly reduced in line with the fall in the price of domestic products there might be a serious growth of unemployment.

An exactly similar difficulty would arise if the government were to decide that it must raise more revenue by way of indirect taxes. The purpose of such a fiscal measure is to reduce purchasing power by raising prices relatively to spendable incomes. Just as in the case of a rise in the price of imports, it would be demanding an unnecessary degree of flexibility in money wage rates to insist that adjustments of this kind should be made through a prompt reduction of money wage rates rather than by a rise in the cost-of-living index.

The best price index to choose for stabilisation purposes would be one which was specially constructed to cover the selling prices of domestically produced output, excluding from such prices the import content of home production and indirect taxes.[1]

As an alternative to the stablisation of a price index of

[1] It might be wise to limit the index to cover home-produced manufactures and to exclude services. For technological reasons productivity rises more rapidly in manufactures than in service industries. Suppose that productivity per man-hour is rising by 3 per cent per annum without any rise in the selling prices of manufactures. Then money wage rates in manufacturing can rise by 3 per cent per annum without any rise in wage costs. If there is no increase in productivity in the service industries but wage rates rise there also by 3 per cent per annum to keep in line with wages in manufactures, then the selling prices of services must rise by 3 per cent per annum. If the price of services accounted for one third of the cost-of-living index, the cost-of-living index would be inflated at a rate of 1 per cent per annum, so that, with a 3-per-cent rise in money wage rates, real wages would be rising at a 2-per-cent rate while the price of manufactures would be stabilised. The exclusion of services would thus have allowed some additional upward creep in money wage rates; but the basic purpose would be achieved of introducing some reliable and stable standard of monetary value which limited the overall rate of inflation of the cost of living to a very moderate amount.

C

domestically produced goods and services, the stabilisation criterion might be to control the total level of demand for home produced goods and services so as to ensure that the national income in monetary terms rose by, say, 5 per cent, but not more than 5 per cent, per annum.

For this purpose the national income would be defined as the sum of all wages, salaries, rents, profits etc., whether earned in free-enterprise or nationalised concerns, such incomes being calculated as the amounts received before the payment of direct taxes (such as income tax). This criterion would also lead to a stable level of the price index of domestically produced goods and services if the total net output of domestically produced goods and services were rising at the same steady rate of 5 per cent per annum either because of increased output per head or of an increase in the total employed labour force. The cost of living would thus rise in so far as (1) the price of imports rose relatively to the price of home-produced goods, (2) the level of indirect taxes on goods and services were raised, or (3) the general level of the net output of home produced goods and services rose by less than 5 per cent per annum. If, for example, total production rises by, say, only 3 per cent, then the price index of domestically produced goods must rise by some 2 per cent, if the producers of these goods and services are to increase by 5 per cent the incomes received from the sale of their output. But there could not with this criterion be any immoderate rates of price inflation or deflation.

The above are two possible criteria for monetary stabilisation : a stabilised price index or a stabilised rate of growth of total money incomes. No doubt other possible candidates could be put forward. The really important point, however, is not so much the exact nature of the criterion as that there should be some reliable, simple, and widely accepted criterion which rules out immoderate price inflations or deflations.[1]

---

[1] One criterion which is sometimes put forward is that the total stock of money in the community should be controlled and increased only at some moderate steady rate of, say, 5 per cent per annum. The present author considers this to be a much less satisfactory criterion because (for example, as a result of budgetary changes) total money expenditures can fluctuate very greatly even though the stock of money is stabilised. Money can circulate more or less rapidly and transactions can be financed by means of substitutes for money, such as extended trade credits. It would seem better to go to the root of the matter and exercise some control both by monetary measures (e.g. changes in the stock of money) and by fiscal measures (e.g. rates of tax) over the total level of monetary expenditures in the economy.

But have the authorities at their command the necessary instruments of control in order to damp down or to stimulate the general level of monetary expenditures in order to ensure the fulfilment of whatever criterion is chosen for the purpose of monetary stabilisation? We must consider not only whether the authorities can raise or lower expenditures by a sufficient amount but also whether they can make such adjustments sufficiently promptly. For speed is at least as important as size of response.

Inflations and deflations of demand largely feed upon themselves. If prices and profits start on an upward movement, this may well lead to an anticipation of a still further rise; and this speculative optimism may cause a further increase in demand which will itself drive prices and profits up still more. If it had been possible by a prompt mechanism of control to nip the incipient inflation in the bud, then the inflationary pressures might never have gathered force. An early control of inflation of demand is likely to require considerably less powerful intervention than a delayed control.

Prompt action is thus desirable. On the other hand it is conceivable that delayed action will actually make matters worse. Suppose that there is a six months' delay in the authorities' response to a change in the economic climate. Consider in these circumstances a situation in which the economic system is naturally moving from the bottom of a recession into a period of economic expansion. The fact that the authorities' reflationary measures will be at their maximum six months after the bottom of the recession, when recovery has had that much time to gather force, might set in motion speculative forces of expansion which would turn a moderate and useful recovery into an undesirable inflation.

Prompt action is thus essential. But nothing succeeds like success. If the authorities announce their firm intention to stabilise a suitable price index or a suitable rate of growth of total money incomes and if they succeed in convincing the public that they can and will enforce this policy, then the forces of speculation will make the authorities' task easier rather than more difficult. For if prices or incomes started to rise above the permitted level, speculators would now expect, not a further rise, but a decline back to the stabilised level. They would thus speculate on a fall rather than a rise in prices and for this reason they would delay purchases rather than speed them up.

But however desirable prompt action may be, some delay between any fluctuation in prices or incomes and the corrective

action is inevitable. First, there will be delay between the actual
fluctuation and its realisation by the authorities. Second, there
may well be administrative and political causes for delay between
the realisation of the fluctuation and the taking of counter-
measures. Third, there will be some delay between the taking of
the counter-measures and the full development of the actual
effects of these counter-measures upon the level of monetary
expenditures and thus upon the level of prices and incomes.

The first of these delays can be reduced only by the prompt
statistical reporting and analysis of changes in prices and incomes.
But the authorities can also be forewarned of the probability
of future changes by the prompt statistical reporting and economic
analysis of all the main relevant economic variables – employment,
unemployment, output, sales, stocks, imports, exports etc. Such
prompt reporting of actual changes may usefully be supplemented
by information about probable future changes, such as information
on producer's present plans for future expenditure on capital
developments.

As far as the delay between the realisation of the need for action
and the actual change of policy is concerned, monetary policy can
score high marks. At any time, without any delay, the Central
Bank can raise or lower the interest rate at which it will lend
funds. It can pump new money into the capital market by the
purchase of securities for new money, or can drain money from
the capital market by selling its own holdings of securities and
cancelling the money which it receives from these sales.

But in so far as the lag between such a change in policy
and its actual effect upon the economy is concerned, monetary
policy scores relatively badly. The Central Bank's action in raising
interest rates and selling securities to drain money out of the
capital market will reduce the liquidity of the commercial banks;
and this will induce the latter to reduce their advances to industry.
But this process takes time and consists of the banks being less
willing to grant new overdrafts, of increasing pressure on clients
to repay their outstanding borrowings, and of negotiating reduc-
tions in the limits of unused overdraft facilities. But meanwhile
businesses may make increased use of existing unused overdraft
facilities and, by paying their bills less promptly, may substitute
trade credits from each other for bank loans. The sale of securities
by the banks together with the banks' restriction of credits combined with their direct raising of interest rates on bank loans will
raise long-term interest rates and make it more difficult and
expensive to raise long-term capital funds. But any effects which

this may have upon expenditures upon capital developments are likely to be delayed, since dearer money is likely to affect projects which are now being planned for future execution rather than the fulfilment of projects on which funds are already being spent.

As far as budgetary policy is concerned, changes in public expenditure score badly from the point of view of both the types of delay now under discussion. Changes in rates of expenditure on public services require considerable reconsideration of the various public policies involved and are likely to involve considerable delays for political discussion and decision. Moreover, even when a decision has finally been taken to change the level of some government expenditure the consequential change in that level is likely to mature only gradually as the new plan replaces the old.

Changes in rates of taxation could probably be devised to score well on both types of delay. So long, however, as tax changes remain a matter of financial legislation they are confined to an annual budget or, at the best, to the presentation of a special budget. In this case they are subject to long delay between the realisation of the need for action and the decision to take action. However, this delay can be removed by granting power under budgetary legislation for certain tax rates to be raised or lowered by a certain percentage at any time that this is required in the interests of stabilisation. And certain taxes can administratively be raised or lowered promptly once the decision is taken. This is true of many indirect taxes. It could also be true of a revised system of income tax. In Chapter VI we shall discuss at length a reform of the system of taxation designed for the more equal distribution of personal incomes. This reform involves the imposition of a high uniform rate of tax on all incomes or on all expenditures for consumption;[1] and such uniform rates of tax could in fact be changed rapidly without any undue administrative complication.

Such changes in taxation are likely to have relatively prompt effects upon the level of personal expenditures. A change in the level of income tax deducted at the source would immediately effect the take-home pay or other income of all citizens. A change in rates of indirect taxation will promptly affect the price which all consumers must pay for the goods in question. It is, of course, probable that some part of the impact effect of such changes may fall upon the savings of the income earners rather than upon their consumption, in which case to this extent there will be no imme-

[1] See pages 89–98 below.

diate effect upon the amounts of goods which they purchase. But the change is likely to affect real expenditure fairly quickly.

It may at first sight appear simple, given prompt use of effective instruments, to control total money expenditures in the desired manner. But this is not so. The economic process in a developed, industrialised country is a complicated system of interrelationships. An increase in incomes will after a time lag lead to an increase in the demand for goods and services which in turn after some time lag is likely to lead to some further increase in incomes paid out to wage earners and other producers of these goods and services. Increases in expenditure are likely to cause at first some fall in stocks and subsequently some increases in prices and, after another time lag, some increase in amounts produced and put on the market for sale. The rate at which the production of goods is growing may itself influence the amount which is spent in buying new machines and in building up stocks of raw materials and semi-finished goods, in order to keep capital equipment and stocks in balance with a higher rate of output. These are only examples; there are in fact many more dynamic relationships of this kind between movements of prices, costs, profits, wages, tax payments, savings, consumption, investment, output, employment, amounts of money, interest rates, imports, exports, foreign capital movements, foreign exchange rates, and so on.

We do not yet know enough about these dynamic relationships to be certain about the precise effect of particular stabilising devices. Suppose that we take a single simple criterion (such as the divergence of selling prices above or below a stated ceiling level or the divergence of the level of money incomes above or below a stated stable growth path) as a guide for the deflationary or inflationary use of certain stabilising devices (such as changes in the supply of money or in surcharges on certain direct or indirect taxes). Then the strength of any disinflationary action should almost certainly depend not only on the extent to which prices or incomes exceed the target level, but also upon the length of time for which they have persisted above that level and upon the rate at which they are still rising. If, to take one example, prices or incomes are too high but are already falling, it may be time to relax the disinflationary pressure in order to make sure that the fall in prices or incomes does not overshoot the mark. It may be that when we know much more than we do at present about the nature of reactions within our dynamic economy, it will be possible to invent an effective automatic formula for stabilisation in which the level of any special stabilisation levies are made to depend automatically on the size, the rate of growth, and the past extent of the divergence between the actual and the target levels of prices or incomes. But for the time being at least those who are in charge of stabilisation devices must be left with some independent discretion by trial and error to use them in the most effective way to achieve the desired stabilisation.

This being the case, there is much to be said in favour of drawing a rather sharp distinction between what may be called the *structural* aspects of budgetary and monetary policies and their *stabilisation* aspects. The structure of the budget and of monetary policy must be planned in the light of the longer-run objectives of the government. Thus budgetary expenditure programmes determine the general structure of the division of the national resources as between the public and the private sectors of the economy. The budgetary programmes for taxation and for expenditures on social security and similar transfer payments must be devised to influence the distribution of incomes and property. The budgetary deficit or surplus of tax revenues over expenditure must be devised, in close co-ordination with monetary policy, to achieve the desired balance between consumption and investment in the community. Thus if the government aims at reducing consumption in order that more of the community's resources should be devoted to investment in capital equipment, it must plan for heavier taxation and a higher budget surplus combined with an easier monetary policy. The higher rates of taxation will discourage private consumption and will lead to public savings through the excess of budgetary revenue over expenditure; and the easier monetary policy will provide the necessary incentive for private enterprise to borrow these savings to invest in capital development.

All these are matters for fairly long-range planning in annual budgets. Of course, in any such annual budget the general level of the budgetary revenues and expenditures, together with the general guide lines for monetary policy, must be planned with a view to achieving that level of total monetary expenditures in the future which is required for stabilisation purposes. But the future can never be foreseen precisely; and, as we have seen, prompt stabilisation adjustments may be necessary from week to week between the annual budgetary planning sessions. There is much to be said for hiving off these week-to-week adjustments from the direct control of parliament and the ordinary executive arm of the government, just as, in fact, day-to-day adjustments of monetary policy by the Central Bank are already hived off subject to a general framework of governmental control over the major lines of monetary policy.

Such a development would require the institution of a Stabilisation Commission under the direction of a board of independent wise men. Such a board would necessarily include the Governor of the Central Bank or his deputy. It would be given the power to impose, within prescribed limits, positive or negative surcharges on certain specified direct and indirect taxes and to determine week-to-week changes in the supply of monetary funds to the capital market through the Central Bank. It would be under a statutory obligation to take these measures with the sole object of raising or damping down the general level of monetary expenditures to the extent necessary to keep the designated price index at its stable predetermined level or to keep the level of total money incomes on its designated growth path.

So much for the mechanisms of stabilisation. We are left with the basic question. Would it lead to mass unemployment? It would obviously do so if, in the middle of a period of rapid inflation, there were a sudden once-for-all introduction of the new stabilisation policy. Suppose money prices and incomes to be rising at highly inflationary rates and suddenly at one point of time total money demand is restricted so as to conform unconditionally to the new stabilisation criterion. The inertia and time lags in the system would undoubtedly mean that there was a sudden reduction in the demand by producers for all inputs including labour. In order to avoid heavy unemployment there would have to be a transitional period during which the policy was being introduced.

A draconian form of transitional policy would be to impose as from a given date an absolute freeze on all money prices and incomes to last for, say, a year or eighteen months, and simultaneously to announce that as from that future date all prices and wage rates would be freed but that budgetary and monetary policies would be ruthlessly devised to control total demand so as to fulfil the given stabilisation criterion.

A gentler form of transition could be arranged through a gradual introduction of the stabilisation criterion. For example if the criterion were the stabilisation of an appropriate price index, this could be achieved by the immediate introduction of the new index of the prices of home produced manufactures, together with a governmental announcement to the effect that from now on monetary and fiscal controls would be so used as to prevent this index (with a present base of 100) from rising above 115 by the

end of the first year, above 125 by the end of the second year,
and above 130 by the end of third year. Thereafter it would be
stabilised at 130. Plans throughout the economy could then be
adjusted to this gradual tailing off of the rate of price inflation.

A similar process could be adopted if the criterion were the
rate of growth of total money incomes. For example, it could be
announced that from now on monetary and fiscal controls would
be so used that the level of money incomes (with a present base
of 100) would be prevented from rising above 115 by the end
of the first year and 125 by the end of the second year, and thereafter would be kept on a steady 5-per-cent-per-annum growth
path.

A transitional period would be a *sine qua non* for success. But
even with such a transitional adjustment the basic question
remains. Would it involve persistent, heavy unemployment? The
avoidance of this disastrous outcome depends upon reforms for
the fixing of money prices and wage rates; and this will be a
central topic of the two following Chapters.

III

Prices and Wages in a Mixed Economy:
(1) *Responsive Prices*

In order that a policy for the control of inflation of the kind discussed in the previous Chapter should operate effectively without leading to unemployment, money prices (including money wage rates) must be responsive to changes in conditions of supply and demand. Where there is an excess of supply over demand at the current price, then the price must fall; when there is an excess demand, the price must rise.

We define prices as being 'responsive' if they react in this way to the balance between supply and demand.

It is clear that if money prices and wage rates are responsive in this sense, the control of inflation by the means discussed in Chapter II will not lead to any serious or lasting unemployment. If and when the authorities restrain money expenditures (in order to restrain a rise in a general index of prices of home produced products or a growth of money income above a target growth path) this will cause rather more markets for particular goods and for particular employments in particular occupations to experience conditions of excess supplies and rather fewer markets to experience conditions of excess demand. Thus if prices are responsive, the general reaction of producers will be to moderate their prices and of wage earners to moderate their wage claims. There would be a moderation of the tendencies for the general index of prices and the general index of total money incomes to rise. The inflationary tendencies would be curbed without any marked or lasting reduction in the general level of output and employment.

There is a second general advantage to be gained from a régime of responsive prices in addition to the fact that it makes practicable a control over the *absolute* general level of money prices and incomes. The adjustment of particular prices and incomes – downwards where there is excess supply and upwards where there is excess demand – causes *relative* prices and incomes to behave in such a way as to attract resources to their most effective economic uses. This influence can be at work in all sectors of the economy. Prices will be high where there is a scarcity of a particular good or service in a particular use, and low where there is a superfluity; and prices will thus act as signals to attract an increase in supplies and to impose economies in use where prices are relatively high and where scarcities exist, and to discourage supply and to encourage an expanded use where superfluities exist.

If, for example, consumers' tastes change and they demand more milk and less bread the relatively high price of milk and low price of bread will attract productive resources from the latter to the former line of production. At the same time as this process of agricultural reorganisation is taking place the low price of bread will restimulate its consumption and the high price of milk will restrain the expansion in its consumption. Or, to take another example, if copper becomes scarce relatively to aluminium, the rise in the price of the former relative to the latter will give the proper incentive to the users of raw materials to substitute the plentiful for the scarce material as well as giving the proper incentives to the producers to expand the production of the scarce relatively to the plentiful material. Or if land becomes scarce and expensive relatively to the cost of labour, producers will search for new techniques of production which use little of the expensive land relatively to labour. And so on throughout the economy. Flexible prices lead to an efficient use of scarce resources.

Labour is, of course, a very special case, and there are many ways in which it should not be treated just like any other commodity – for the very simple reason that the whole purpose of the economy is to promote the welfare of men and women and not that of bricks and mortar. Men and women and children should be generously supported in childhood, sickness, unemployment, old age, and other times of dependent need. Chapters V and VI will be devoted to a discussion of radical fiscal and similar measures outside the wage system designed to promote these welfare needs and in general to achieve a much more equal distribution of income and wealth, which should not be determined simply by the forces of supply and demand in the labour market.

But if such fiscal measures are adequately developed to look after the distribution of income and wealth, a system whereby wage rates responded to conditions of supply and demand in particular labour markets would not be unjust; and it would serve the double purpose of enabling the authorities to control inflation without causing unemployment and of promoting the employment of labour in the most productive uses.

If the authorities had to restrict total demand to prevent a general inflation of prices and incomes, the resulting temporary excess supplies in various markets would restrict the demand for labour. But if this led to a moderation of wage demands in those markets in which there was a threat of an excess supply of labour, the result would not be any lasting unemployment, but a reduction in the growth of money wage-costs. Producers would be in a position to restrain their selling prices without restricting their production.

Moreover, in these conditions relative wage-rates as between different skills, regions, occupations, etc., could be used to promote the most productive use of labour, both by inducing individual employers to economise in the use of labour where it is scarce and to make free use of it where it is plentiful, and also by attracting labour from firms where it is in plentiful supply to firms where it is scarce.

In so far as workers cannot move easily between regions and occupations, the first of these functions is very important both for the maintenance of full employment and for ensuring the most economic use of available labour resources. If computer programmers are scarce, it is important that they should be used only on the most important and productive tasks; and a high cost for employing a computer programmer will help to cut out wasteful uses of scarce ability. If unskilled workers are available in large numbers in a particular market, it is important that useful tasks which they could perform should not be made unprofitable by a high cost for the employment of such workers.

But it is important to promote the movement of workers from employment of low, to employments of high, social productivity. The incentive to move from a sector where pay is low to a sector where pay is high may well be less powerful than the incentive to move from a sector where there is unemployment to a sector where job opportunities are good. But this latter type of movement does not necessarily imply movement from points of low to points of high productivity. Job opportunities for new entrants may be poor in a highly paid occupation just because entry into the occupation is artificially restricted and the wage of labour is maintained there at an artificially high level, with the result that employers restrict their demand for workers; and in consequence job opportunities may be better where wages are depressed and, as a result, the demand for labour is high. The more readily relative wages can be allowed to respond to true rather than artificial scarcities and surpluses of labour, the less likely are such situations to arise and the more nearly will opportunities for employment be equalised in all sectors. But the more nearly this position of equal job opportunities in all sectors is realised, the more important will differences in pay become relatively to differences in job opportunities in attracting labour from depressed to prosperous occupations.

Thus a system in which wages and prices are responsive to supply-demand conditions would serve the twofold purpose of enabling monetary and budgetary policies to be designed to avoid inflation without causing unemployment and also to attract resources into the most productive uses. But can such price and wage flexibility be achieved, and, if so, by what means?

One method of achieving flexibility is the restoration of competitive conditions in the markets concerned. Effective competitive conditions are, however, practicable only in those cases in which any one seller of a good or service is liable to potential undercutting from an alternative seller of the good or service if the price is unduly raised; and in which any one buyer is liable to potential outbidding by an alternative buyer if the price which he offers is unduly low.

Solutions on these lines, where they are possible, bring with them further great social advantages. Competitive conditions of this kind ensure that there shall not be great concentrations of power in the economy and thus they help to safeguard individual liberty and freedom of choice. If a consumer does not like A's product, he can buy B's instead. If a worker does not like employer C, he can seek work with employer D. Moreover, no single employer and no single labour union can boss the individual citizen and tyrannise over his behaviour.

Workable competitive conditions are not possible in all markets. In some cases very large-scale operations are necessary in order to produce efficiently; and for such technical reasons it is not possible to have competing units in a single market. One has only to think of a road network, or a railway network, or a telephone network, or a network for the supply of electricity on a national grid, or the supply of water and the disposal of sewage in a town, to realise that these cases in which effective competition is impossible are quite frequent. But in many cases there are no technical obstacles to the promotion of workable competitive conditions. And in any case monopoly and competition are matters of degree. For example, even though gas, electricity, railways, and road networks must be monopolies, their activities can be so arranged that gas may compete with electricity and road transport with rail transport. Competition of this indirect kind is very imperfect; but it can serve seriously to curtail the monopoly power of the alternative sources of supply.

There is, however, a horrifying tendency in our present society to allow, indeed to encourage, the formation of huge monopolistic concentrations of power which are not necessary on technical grounds and which are subject to a minimum of social control. Giant industrial concerns may be formed and achieve great market power and undue political influence, even though the technical production advantages of unified control on so gigantic a scale are not very great. Labour unions in essential occupations may be able to insist upon the pay and conditions which they judge for themselves to be appropriate and, in some cases, even to determine what government shall be allowed to pass what legislation. A corporate state made up of huge giant industrial concerns and labour monopolies, rejecting social control, openly or by hidden pressure influencing and sometimes defying democratic parliamentary government, and independently of each other scrambling for power and economic status is the hideous reality with which we are at present threatened.

What can we do to be saved? The remainder of this Chapter will be devoted to a brief survey of the kind of measures which might be taken to restore the flexible operation of a responsive price mechanism in the case of product prices. In the following Chapter we will turn to the problem of making wage rates more responsive.

Some measures might be taken to discourage large-sized and to encourage small-sized industrial concerns. There is no sharp, clear-cut distinction to be drawn between the absence or the presence of economies of large-scale production. Economies of large scale may exist; but if only small economies are to be gained from very large-scale operations, it may be desirable to sacrifice the economies (real though they may be) in order to gain the other real advantages of smaller-scale competition discussed earlier in this Chapter. It is a matter of degree. The intelligent radical will, however, put a relatively high value on the dispersal of power over many relatively small-scale independent units. The following are six possible measures to encourage small-scale and discourage large-scale operations.

(1) The present Corporation Tax which is levied on the profits of all companies might be abolished and replaced by a progressive tax on the numbers employed by a single employer. Concerns employing less than a certain number of employees would escape

tax altogether. Concerns employing more employees would pay a tax on this excess number. Concerns employing still more men would pay a tax at a still higher rate on this further excess of numbers. And so on up the scale of employment.

(2) Profits which were not distributed in dividends might be subjected to a special tax, if the amount so put to reserve by a single company exceeded some stated amount. Small firms could grow by putting undistributed profit to reserve without taxation; but such a tax would discourage further growth through the ploughing back of their own profits by firms which were already large. The distribution of their profits in dividends would mean that large firms must grow by appealing to the capital market for new funds, while individual savings from their distributed profits would be available on the capital market for the finance of other firms.

(3) The taxation of profits put to reserve by large firms could be combined with the development of special institutions to borrow savings on the capital market in order to lend to small firms. A number of such special semi-public bodies might be set up with government guarantees of their borrowings and possibly with some measure of direct government subsidy. They would be instructed to make it their job to seek out and to finance the formation and the development of efficient and promising firms employing less than a stated number of workers.

(4) Company Law might be revised to limit the holding by one company of shares in another company in such a way as to prevent networks of control whereby holding companies own and control a large number of subsidiary companies or one company is part owner and controller of another company. True economies of large-scale production could still be achieved but only by the growth of a single unified company.

(5) The control of mergers and take-over of the assets of one company by another might be submitted to more rigorous supervision with the sole purpose of preventing such mergers which threatened to reduce competitive conditions unless there were overwhelming advantages to be reaped from the larger scale of operations. Such monopoly control might well be extended to insist on the break-up of giant concerns which operated many separate plants and activities, wherever it was judged that such plants and activities could be independently operated without any overwhelming loss of productive efficiency.

(6) Research and development and the patenting of inventions present a basic dilemma in a competitive economy. Invention,

innovation, and the production of new ideas is a costly process. But once the new idea has been produced it is from society's point of view a costless good. If I eat this particular loaf of bread, you cannot eat it. But if I make use of a particular new idea in building my machine, that presents no real obstacle to you also making use of this same new idea in building your machine; yet the persons who invented the idea and developed its practical application used up real resources of their time, tools, materials, etc. in doing so. From the ideal social point of view, therefore, inventors, innovators, and developers should be paid for the production of new ideas; but once the new ideas were produced they should be at the free disposal of all who wanted to use them, since their use by A presents no real obstacle to their use by B.

This feature of research and development provides a very strong argument in favour of large-scale productive organisations. A small firm may have to spend as much as a large firm to produce a given innovation, but it will have a much smaller output over which to spread the benefits of the new idea. A large firm has a large output over which to spread the benefits from its overhead expenditure on research and development. It is true that patent arrangements may allow a small firm or even an individual innovator to charge other firms for the use of a new idea, thus indirectly reaping the reward from the spreading of the benefits of the new idea over a large production by other firms. But patent arrangements have two disadvantages : by charging patent fees they restrict the use of new ideas which, as we have seen, is really socially costless once the idea has been produced; and they may enable powerful large-scale monopolies to be built up on the basis of a series of innovations for the use of which the single large-scale producer holds the exclusive patent rights.

Accordingly, if it is desired to make small-scale operations efficient, there is a strong case for governmental measures to promote research and development in such ways that the resulting innovations can be freely used by competing small-scale producers. Such measures might include : (1) research and development by a number of governmental institutions financed directly by the State, the fruits of whose work would be at the free disposal of anyone who wished to make use of the innovations; (2) the promotion, perhaps with some element of governmental subsidy, of co-operative research institutes, jointly financed by all the producers in a particular industry, the fruits of whose work could be freely used by any member of the research co-operative; (3) legislation entitling any producer to use any patented process provided that he paid a fair royalty for its use – the appropriate rate of royalty being open to some form of impartial arbitration; and (4) in those cases where it would be considered a helpful means to promote small-scale competitors, the taking of powers by the government on the payment of fair compensation to acquire any particular patent rights and to make the use of the innovation free to all comers.

The measures which we have discussed so far are all designed to promote small-scale rather than large-scale productive organisations. There are, however, further measures which, regardless of the scale of the productive enterprises, can be taken to promote the influence of price competition in any given market. The following are some instances of this type of measure.

(1) Measures may be taken to prohibit various restrictive practices by producers, for example, cartel agreements binding otherwise independent suppliers not to produce more than certain agreed quantities or not to charge less than certain agreed prices; or the requirement by a producer of a particular product that his customers should purchase no competing supplies of that product from any other supplier; or a requirement by a producer that any trader to whom he sold should not resell the product below a certain stated price : trading practices of this kind can be made illegal. In fact since World War II there has been much advance in the United Kingdom along these lines.

(2) One of the most effective ways of promoting price competition would be to permit the completely free import of products from foreign suppliers. An efficient scale of production of a single firm in some cases represents a very large proportion of the total United Kingdom market. But at the same time it may represent a small proportion of the total world production of the product. Competition with foreign suppliers is thus one of the most important reasons for the restoration of a free-trade policy for the United Kingdom. We will return to this problem in Chapters VIII and IX when we come to discuss the implications for international economic and financial policies of the domestic policies which we are advocating.

(3) Much might be achieved by means of a substantial tax on advertisement. Of course, much advertisement of an informative nature is necessary and desirable. But much advertisement is not of this kind. A tax on advertisement would increase the incentive for firms to seek markets by cutting prices rather than by persuasive bamboozlement. Moreover, persuasive advertisement may irrationally bind particular customers to particular brands

of a product produced by a particular firm. This may make competition by a newcomer to the industry more difficult and thus impede the competitive growth of more efficient newcomers.

(4) A return to a system of broadcasting which is not based upon commercial advertisement. If it is desired to avoid a monopoly of television, there is no reason why there should not be a number of independent corporations like the British Broadcasting Corporation broadcasting competing programmes.

(5) Measures might be taken to replace much interested persuasive advertisement with impartial information through the promotion by the State of bodies for consumers' research and education. The provision and widespread dissemination by a number of independent semi-public bodies of information about the real qualities of different products would increase the forces of the market mechanism to which the producers would have to submit.

But when all reasonable measures have been taken to encourage smaller-scale enterprises and to promote price competition many cases will remain where large-scale production and substantial monopoly powers remain. In these cases there are only two possible acceptable lines of policy.

First, selling prices may be subjected to some form of official control whereby the producers concerned are compelled to charge prices which are in line with their costs but which, in view of their market power, are lower than it would be in their interest to charge if they were uncontrolled. A permanent system of detailed governmental control over all selling prices is both impracticable and undesirable for the reasons already discussed (page 30 above); and indeed the measures for the promotion of small-scale enterprise and for the promotion of market forces which we have discussed in this Chapter are designed for the very purpose of making the market rather than the bureaucrat restrain prices. But cases will remain where the market will not be sufficiently powerful and the aid of the bureaucrat will have to be invoked. Government departments might be empowered to refer to some body such as the Monopolies Commission the question whether in a particular case a particular producer was charging prices which represented undesirable monopolistic profit margins. If such were ruled to be the case, the producer in question would be required to reduce his prices accordingly. In carrying out this function the relevant government departments would be ready to receive complaints of unduly high prices from any member of the public, but they might also be aided by the institution of a consumers' council whose express duty it would be to bring such cases to their notice.

The second and final solution is the social ownership and management of the activities concerned. Railways, roads, gas, electricity, sewage, water supply, telephones, are all examples where price competition in a free market is out of the question. But the whole discussion in this Chapter has been based upon the desirability of making prices responsive to conditions of supply and demand. From this point of view there is little purpose in nationalising various activities unless after nationalisation the concerns are operated in a way which makes their prices responsive to changes in supply-demand conditions. The detailed application of this principle raises technical issues which it is not possible to discuss in this short book. But certain general principles may be mentioned.

The first obvious principle is that nationalised concerns should not be protected from direct or indirect competition from outside sources. If a private producer can compete with the product of a nationalised industry, he should be permitted to do so. Nor should indirect competition be prevented. Thus imports of a substitute product should not be restricted simply to protect prices, output, and employment in a nationalised industry which is producing a particular domestic product. In so far as outside substitutes exist in the private-market sector of the economy, they should be allowed to play their part in setting the price-cost framework within which the nationalised sector must operate.

Within this framework the nationalised concerns should adjust their prices to correspond with the demand and supply conditions for their products. There are two different general methods for such adjustments, one of which will be suitable in some cases and the other in other cases but both of which result ultimately in the desired response of prices to supply-demand conditions. The first method is to raise (or lower) the selling price according as demand exceeds (or falls short of) supply, but to expand (or contract output according as the resulting selling price exceeds (or falls short of) the cost of production. The second method is to expand (or contract) output according as demand exceeds (or falls short of) supply, but to raise (or lower) the selling price according as the resulting cost of production is above (or below) the existing selling price. Both methods move prices and outputs towards the equilibrium levels at which the amount supplied is equal to the amount demanded and at the same time the price is equal to the cost of production.

Problems arise, however, in deciding what is the relevant cost of production. A socialised concern should take into account all the social costs involved. For example, any costs to outsiders due to the nationalised concern's pollution of the environment should be brought into account, even though a private enterprise might be able to avoid paying for them. This sort of problem will be discussed in more detail in Chapter VII below.

But there is a rather more technical question of the definition of costs to be taken into account. Consider a nationalised railway system. It will have a large fixed capital equipment or permanent way consisting of lines, embankments, tunnels, stations, signalling equipment, etc. On this permanent way it can operate more or less traffic. In such conditions there is likely to be a considerable difference between the marginal cost of carrying a small additional amount of traffic (the extra fuel, rolling stock, maintenance work, manpower, etc. involved) and the average cost of carrying all its traffic (i.e. the interest on its fixed equipment as well as the manning costs, spread over the whole of its traffic). But it is the marginal cost (i.e. the cost added by taking on a little more traffic) rather than the average cost of the existing traffic which measures the extra strain on the community's resources due to taking on the last extra units of traffic. It would, therefore, as a general principle, seem appropriate that those who are operating the system in the interests of the community should charge to the consumers a price equal to the marginal cost rather than the average cost of the service which they are providing.

This may mean running the nationalised concern at an abnormally high profit or running it at a loss.

Suppose that a nationalised railway line is already heavily congested. To charge for each unit of traffic on it a price which will cover all the additional costs due to adding that unit of traffic to the already congested line may be to charge a price considerably above the average cost of traffic on the line. Indeed, at the extreme it may be literally impossible to add more traffic on the existing permanent way, in which case a price must be charged high enough to restrict the demand for traffic to the capacity level of the existing permanent way, and this price may well exceed the average cost of operating the system. In small-scale competitive industry this could not continue for long, because some further small-scale plant would be attracted by the abnormally high profit to deal with the additional traffic at a cost not much different from the existing average cost. But on the railway this will not necessarily be economic. To expand the fixed equipment of the industry to deal with the increased traffic might mean duplicating much of the structure of railway lines, embankments, tunnels, etc., and while there may be more traffic than can very easily be taken on the existing line, there may not be enough additional traffic to make economic the minimum extension which is technically possible. It may be economically desirable, therefore, to go on indefinitely charging for traffic a price which will be sufficient to keep the demand down to what can be handled on the existing line, even though this price is well above average cost and thus results in a considerable and permanent extra profit.

Conversely, if the demand for traffic is not large enough fully to utilise the existing line, it will be economic to charge for each unit of traffic a price which merely covers the additional running expenses incurred by taking that unit of traffic on to the existing railway system, even though this price does not cover the average cost of operation. In small-scale competitive industry this also would not last for long, since little by little units of capital equipment on which a loss was being made would go out of production by not being replaced as they wore out. But in the case of the railway the choice may be between a drastic reduction of capital equipment (e.g. using a single instead of a double track) or maintaining it on its present scale; and while there may be too much essential traffic to make it economical to make the minimum contraction of equipment which is technically possible, there may not be enough traffic to enable the existing system to be operated to the full.

There are, however, in any case a number of applications of the marginal cost system which are clearly desirable and which do not necessarily lead to operation of the concern at a permanent profit or loss. An obvious example in the case of the generation of electricity is to charge a higher price for electricity consumed at times of peak demand than for electricity consumed during off-peak periods. The marginal cost of producing electricity at peak periods (when the less economic generating units must be called in to supplement the more economic units) is much higher than the marginal cost at off-peak periods. To charge higher on-peak prices and lower off-peak prices is the appropriate way of giving the correct degree of incentive to all consumers to rearrange the timing of their demands so as to shift demand from electricity supplied at a high marginal cost to electricity supplied at a low marginal cost.

But this raises a further problem of pricing. The administration of a sophisticated pricing system is itself costly. There would be certain gain from charging higher on-peak than off-peak prices, if the charging system were costless. But if it involved the production and maintenance of expensive metering devices and if the gain from the more sophisticated charging system were not great, it might be preferable to stay with the cruder system of a uniform charge for on-peak and off-peak consumption. There are innumerable instances of this balancing of costs and benefits in sophisticated, flexible pricing systems. Should meters be introduced to measure the domestic consumption of water? Could motor vehicles be charged for the use of the roads according to the likely congestion on particular roads at particular times of day in a particular direction?

The intelligent radical, being intelligent, will recognise that perfect adjustment of prices to conditions of demand-needs and supply-costs is not possible, but, being a radical, he will wish to extend the field of flexible, responsive price adjustment as far as can be done without undue cost.

IV

Prices and Wages in a Mixed Economy:
(2) *Responsive Wages*

The intelligent radical will realise that we have now reached the crucial question. Can wages and salaries be made sufficiently responsive to supply-demand conditions? Let us go back to our starting point. Suppose that it were decided that the financial authorities should so control the level of total monetary expenditures as to stabilise the level of prices or the growth of money incomes. The consequential restraint of demand for the products of industry would lead to unemployment of labour if there were no corresponding restraint to the demand for increased wages. But if this restraint in the demand for labour did lead to a sufficiently responsive restraint in demands for higher money wage rates, then no unemployment need result; and at the same time there would be a continuing rise in real wage rates at as high a rate as increased productivity made possible.

Keynesian methods for a stabilising control over the total money demand for goods and services combined with responsiveness of individual money prices and wage rates to market conditions is the intelligent radical's prescription for combining price stability with full employment. But is it possible to achieve an adequate responsiveness of wages?

We have made proposals (pages 40–41 above) for measures to ease the transition from present inflationary conditions to a future state of monetary stabilisation. But there is every reason to fear that even so, unless there were some appropriate changes in existing institutional arrangements for the determination of rates of pay, such a stabilisation policy might well result in a markedly higher level of unemployment than is necessary or acceptable.

It is, of course, impossible to reduce unemployment literally to zero. There will always be some persons who are leaving one job and looking for another either because they wish to move or else because of economic changes which have made some jobs in one region or occupation or industry redundant even though increased vacancies are appearing in other regions or occupations or industries. We shall return later (pages 63–65 below) to consider the desirability of measures to ease such movements of men and women from one task to another, the success of which will diminish the small amount of inevitable unemployment which is necessary to allow for change in a dynamic economy.

But with present institutional arrangements for the setting of wages and salaries it is quite possible that unemployment might have to be considerably above this inescapable minimum in order to exercise the necessary restraint on claims for increases in money pay. Presumably there is some level of trade depression and of unemployment which would sufficiently reduce the power of trade unions and similar bodies of workers to claim wage increases and which would sufficiently diminish the power and willingness of employers to grant wage increases. But no one would willingly accept massive unemployment as a solution to the problem. Are there any more acceptable solutions?

One possibility is to attempt a full-scale detailed bureaucratic control over all rates of pay. This involves, first, laying down criteria to determine the legitimacy of wage increases and, second, instituting some governmental machinery to see that these criteria are observed. Such a procedure will not be attractive to the intelligent radical; and in any case it is probably quite impracticable as a permanent solution. The criteria must cover such matters as productivity agreements, the treatment of very low wages, the correction of acute shortages of labour in particular sectors of the economy, the maintenance of equitable differentials, and so on. The effective application of these criteria to basic rates and to over-time rates, to piece rates and to hourly rates, to fringe benefits and working hours, in the case of men, women, and juveniles of different skills over a wide range of occupations and industries in a large number of firms in different regions and localities would involve a most far-reaching incursion of governmental control into the whole of the private, free-enterprise sector of the economy. Some rough-and-ready overall crude control (such as a freeze of every wage rate) may be practicable as a short-run emergency measure; but experience suggests that the degree of detailed, sophisticated control that would be necessary as a permanent measure to maintain an acceptable degree of fairness and efficiency in a dynamic economy is not really a practical possibility.

Another possibility is to work for what is known as a voluntary incomes policy, that is to say, to hand over this formidable task not to a governmental institution but to some central body composed of representatives of employers and workers, such as the TUC and the CBI, to be hammered out by them as a joint bargaining decision. The intelligent radical will find this solution equally unattractive; and it is probably equally impracticable. Even if it could be worked, it would mean that what were in essence public rules and regulations of the most far-reaching importance to the individual workers and employers concerned were determined by the decisions of two private monopolistic organisations in no way responsible to the democratically elected government. If the TUC and the CBI had the power over their members to make this solution possible, they would be usurping powers which in the intelligent radical's opinion properly belong to the government.

The remaining possibility is frankly to recognise the fact that trade unions and similar professional organisations are monopolistic organisations in which individuals have banded together to fix a price for what they are selling and have acquired a practically unlimited legal right to hold society to ransom by a joint, monopolistic refusal to operate on terms other than those which they have themselves decided to be right and proper in their own interests. Such uncontrolled monopolistic bargaining power is excessive.

The fact that trade unions are monopolistic organisations does not, of course, imply that they should cease to exist; but it does imply that, like all other monopolies, they should not refuse to accept certain social controls over their activities. Monopolistic organisation for some purposes is inevitable, indeed desirable. The intelligent radical recognises this, even though he would like to see as much freedom for private enterprise and trade as is feasible in modern conditions; he would not argue that transport by rail or the generation of electricity should be conducted by a very large number of small competing units. The mere fact that trade unions are monopolistic organisations does not automatically condemn them; and, of course, in fact they perform a number of very important, necessary functions. Many of their most important functions in representing the interests of the workers to the managers on many aspects of the conditions of their work and employment have nothing to do with wage-fixing. Moreover, where there would otherwise be a very large number of workers facing a very small number of employers, trade unions are needed to provide monopolistic bargaining power to offset the monopsonistic, exploitative powers of the limited number of employers.

In the preceding Chapter we have outlined a number of measures which would encourage smaller-scale relatively to larger-scale productive organisations. As a result the number of independent competing employers would increase. The intelligent radical would welcome any tendency for rates of pay to be determined independently within each firm as between each independent employer and an independently organised representation of the particular workers in his employment. The reorganisation of trade union structure to give increased independent influence in wage-fixing to each firm's group of employees would be in the same radical tradition.

But, as we have argued, large-scale production is in many cases inevitable. Even if the principle of matching bargaining power whereby each independent employer was faced with an independent organisation representing his own employees were fully applied, there would of necessity be many large-scale trade unions. The existence of such organised monopolistic bodies is inevitable and indeed desirable. But this does not, of course, imply that there should be no social control over their activities. Indeed, in no other sphere of economic life does one consider it right or proper that a monopolistic organisation should not be subject to social controls of one kind or another over such matters as the price it charges or the amounts it supplies of whatever good or service it is providing.[1]

Can we devise a suitable practical form of control over the excessive use of a trade union's monopolistic powers? The intelligent radical will not want to restrict in any way the freedom of any particular employer to offer any increase in pay which he finds desirable to attract workers to his own particular thriving business. He will wish only to put some restraint on excessive upward pressure on rates of pay in those cases where the demand conditions do not make abrupt increases in pay necessary in order to man up the concern in question.

[1] There is a widespread confusion introduced by the ambiguity of such phrases as 'the right to withdraw labour'. Of course, in a free society any individual worker should be free to decide to give up his present job in order to do something else, just as an individual baker should be free to decide to cease to bake bread in order to do something else. In this sense there is in a free society a basic 'right to withdraw one's labour'. But it is quite a different matter for all the workers in a particular occupation to agree together simultaneously to withdraw their labour as a concerted monopoly action to raise the price of their labour. There should be no more unfettered right in a free society for such concerted withdrawals of labour than for all the bakeries in the country to get together to restrict the output of bread in order to make a monopoly profit on its production. Concerted monopoly action as contrasted with individual action, is a proper subject for social control.

There will in fact be no satisfactory solution of this problem until there is a widespread consensus of opinion among reasonable citizens, both trade unionists and other members of the community, on the reasonableness of some form of social control. Much the best basis for this would be agreement between the trade unions and the relevant associations of employers to take disputes about wage rates to be settled by impartial arbitration. The arbitrators would be required to decide whether the rise in pay which was in dispute was or was not needed (in the absence of unnecessary restrictions on entry into the occupation in question) to make the occupation sufficiently remunerative relatively to other occupations to attract men and workers to the work in question on the scale which would be needed to meet the future demands for their services.

But in the absence of a completely universal voluntary acceptance of such a procedure some social control over industrial action is necessary as a final safeguard. The following is one possible set of arrangements which might serve this purpose.

(1) The government lays dawn from time to time a 'norm' for the annual percentage rise in wage earnings. We will speak of this norm as x per cent per annum for the time being and will leave to later consideration the problem of deciding upon its level.

(2) Any group of employers and employees would, however, be perfectly free to reach agreement on any wage or salary bargain, whether or not it implied a rise of earnings above the x per cent per annum.

(3) There would, however, be a recognised system of tribunals or courts to which, in the case of a trade dispute about wages or salaries, the matter could be referred in order to obtain a judgement as to whether the increase in pay which was claimed did or did not exceed the x-per-cent norm.

The function of these wage tribunals or courts would be very limited, simply and solely to determine whether a particular pay claim would cause the earnings of the workers concerned to be more than x per cent higher than they were a year ago. They would be required to decide whether, taking into account such matters as fringe benefits, hours of work, and the probable effects on overtime, the cost to the employer of employing a given amount of the labour concerned would be raised by more than x per cent. Such a determination might take a little time; and the tribunals would have to be empowered to issue interim judgements which could later be revised by a final determination.

(4) If it were ruled by the tribunal that the claim under con-

sideration exceeded the x-per-cent norm, then, but only then, regulations would come into force to curb the bargaining power of the workers who were pressing the claim. The sort of regulations which might be appropriate would be : that any workers who went on strike or took other industrial action in support of the claim would lose any accumulated rights to redundancy payments in their existing jobs; that any social benefits paid for the support of them or their families during the strike would become a liability of the trade union that was supporting the strike or, failing that, would be treated as a debt of the individual worker concerned; and the trade union would be liable to tax on any strike benefits which it paid out to its members. On the other hand, there would be no curbing of trade unions' bargaining powers in respect of any action which they took in support of claims which did not exceed the x-per-cent norm.

In Chapter VI we shall suggest some far-reaching changes in the present system of taxation and of social security in the interests of ensuring much greater equality in the distribution of income and property. But we will also discuss their application to the problem of the social control of trade union bargaining and we will argue (see page 100 below) that they have the incidental advantage of reinforcing such control. They could be so operated as, on the one hand, to reinforce the restraint of bargaining power in the case of industrial action in support of claims in excess of the x-per-cent norm; but, on the other hand, they would greatly strengthen the bargaining power of trade unions in the case of industrial action in support of claims within the x-per-cent norm.

The choice of the actual number for the x-per-cent norm would give the government an important new weapon for the management of the economy. In the context of a financial policy designed to control the level of total monetary expenditures so as to attain some clearly defined stabilisation target, the general principle on which the x per cent should be determined is clear. If the stabilisation policy were leading to unemployment, that would be evidence that on the average money wage rates were rising too quickly; in this case the level of the x-per-cent norm should be reduced in order to restrict the upward pressure on wage rates. If, on the other hand, the stabilisation policy was tending to result in an excess of unfilled vacancies, there would be evidence that the restraints on bargaining power could be relaxed and the x-per-cent norm could be raised.

It has been suggested on pages 40–41 above that as a start on the transitional path from inflation to stabilisation the target might be to prevent the selected index of prices or income from rising by more than 15 per cent in the first year. To match this an initial x-per-cent norm of 15 per cent might also be set. Such an initial experimental level of 15 per cent would then be open to annual revision. During the transitional period as the permitted rate of rise of selling prices or of incomes was progressively restrained, so the norm for wage increases would be reduced also. By a process of trial and error the wage norm would be relaxed or made more stringent relatively to the permitted rise in prices or incomes, according as this stabilisation policy was achieved with an excess of unfilled vacancies or with a growing threat of unemployment. Ultimately when the régime of complete stabilisation of prices or of the growth of incomes was reached, the wage norm would have been adjusted by this experimental method to an appropriate very moderate level.

A system of the kind discussed above which resulted in wage rates becoming more responsive to conditions of supply and demand would have great advantages from three points of view : the control of inflation, the protection of individual liberties from unnecessary interventions, and the efficient use of economic resources. But what effect would it have upon the distribution of income?

Reforms on the lines suggested in this Chapter would be quite unacceptable unless they were accompanied by an alternative mechanism for controlling the distribution of income. In the next two Chapters we will discuss at length various fiscal and other measures for achieving a much more equal distribution of income and property. The intelligent radical must realise the necessity for a revolutionary change in political attitudes shifting the emphasis from industrial action over wage-fixing to political action over fiscal measures as the recognised means for achieving a more equitable distribution of income.

This shift of emphasis is necessary not only in order to achieve those advantages of more responsive wage rates which we have already discussed in this Chapter; it would be desirable even if the only consideration were the effect on the distribution of income. As a means of achieving a more equitable distribution, appropriate fiscal measures, determined by democratic, parliamentary procedures, could be much more effective than wage bargaining, determined by industrial action.

Pushing up the general level of money wage rates is a very ineffective method for achieving any radical redistribution of income from the rich to the poor. In the first place, not all workers are poor and not all property owners are rich. But, secondly, the method has very strict limits as a means of redistributing income from interest, profits, and rents to wages and salaries. Once sufficient upward pressure on rates of pay has been exerted to counterbalance any monopsonistic exploitative powers by employers, further pressure can only lead *either* to a corresponding inflation of prices, in which case there is no gain in real wages nor loss in real profits, *or* to unemployment, since the rise in real wage costs will make the employment of labour unprofitable.

When one considers the effect of uncontrolled collective bargaining upon relative wages, the instrument is seen to be an even blunter one. There is no reason whatsoever to believe that the worst paid workers will have the greatest bargaining power and, therefore, be able to improve their relative position. Particular groups of workers in essential occupations can hope to get as much as they demand by withdrawing their labour. Small groups of workers producing components which are widely used as essential elements in many other occupations can similarly cause great and widespread economic loss; and their bargaining power will be great, since a rise in pay to their small numbers will not be very costly whereas the threatened loss of their output would bring much other activity to a standstill. Human nature being what it is, it is workers in these sorts of situation who will gain relatively to those who are working in less essential or less sensitive situations. This has nothing to do with an equitable distribution of rewards.

Where a particular group of workers achieves an exceptional increase in pay there are four groups of citizens whose relative real incomes are affected. First, there are the workers who remain in employment in the occupation in question, and these persons gain. They are not necessarily badly paid workers. Second, there are the recipients of the profits of the employing concern, who are likely to lose. But not all recipients of dividends are rich. For example, in the case of a private enterprise concern some of the reduced profit may lead to a reduction in the income of a pension fund whose beneficiaries may not be rich. In the case of a nationalised concern the reduced profit or increased loss will fall on the general body of taxpayers. Third, there is the general body of consumers of the product who are likely to lose in so far as the increased wage cost leads to a rise in the selling price of the product; and the product may be an essential item in the poor man's budget. Finally, there is the often forgotten and ill-defined group of workers who would otherwise have found employment in the occupation in question, but who find themselves unemployed or employed in less attractive and less well-paid jobs as the opportunities for employment in the priviliged occupation are restricted. The final outcome on the distribution of real incomes is thus arbitrary and haphazard. There can be no doubt that fiscal measures, expressly designed to achieve a given redistribution, constitute a superior instrument for this purpose.

A shift of emphasis from wage-fixing to fiscal measures as the basic instrument for controlling the distribution of income is the first necessary condition for the achievement of a system of wages which are responsive to conditions of supply and demand. A second necessary condition is the promotion of conditions which make it easy for workers to move from one employment to another.

In a dynamic economy shifts of demand from one activity to another will continually cause some employments to be expanding and others to be contracting. If movement from one occupation to another is easy, then only a small and temporary rise in unemployment or reduction in pay in the contracting activities relatively to the expanding activities will be needed to effect the necessary readjustment. If movement is difficult, heavier unemployment and larger differences in rates of pay would have to be faced. Clearly a régime of responsive wages would be much more feasible and effective where movement was easy.

Such movement can be eased both by measures designed to bring work to the workers and also by measures designed to bring the workers to the work. The intelligent radical will support both types of measure. In the first group are fiscal devices such as the subsidisation of employment in depressed regions in which unemployment is relatively high and the taxation of employment in regions in which there is an exceptional and acute shortage of labour, thus giving employers an incentive to take work to the workers. In the second group are measures designed to inform workers of alternative job opportunities, to retrain workers for new tasks, and to help meet the costs of removal from one locality to another.

But it is equally important to remove artificial obstacles to the movement of workers. Existing rent controls and other interventions in the housing market obstruct movement from one locality to another; and we will discuss later (pages 69–72 below) reforms which would remove these obstacles to mobility. In addition there are at present many artificial restrictions on the entry of workers into particular occupations. Limitation of entry to a trade to persons trained as apprentices, when the number of apprentices permitted to train is unnecessarily limited or the time and expense of apprenticeship are unduly extended; trade union insistence on pre-entry closed-shop arrangements, whereby only trade unionists may work in a particular sector of industry and the trade union itself limits the number who may join it; professional examination requirements which demand qualifications or time spent in training which are not essential for the proper performance of the professional service; all these and similar restrictive practises may make it impossible or unnecessarily difficult for people to move into particular occupations. An exceptionally high rate of pay to such a group of workers may be needed to restrict the demand to the artificially restricted supply, but the high rate of pay is not needed to attract labour; indeed, it is paid solely because workers who would otherwise be qualified for the job and would be attracted to it are artificially excluded.

The difficult problem is the definition of what qualifications are reasonably needed for a particular job. In many cases where the employer is a business concern which is technically quite capable of judging for itself what skill is necessary and whether any particular applicant has in one way or another acquired that skill, there is really little need for any imposition upon the employer of limitations on his freedom to employ those whom he considers to be suitable, though the employers themselves may well find it useful to judge qualifications on the basis of some recognised process of training and examination. But in some jobs this simple condition may not be fulfilled; for example, in occupations where bad work by one man may endanger the health or safety of fellow workers, a restriction may rightly and properly be imposed upon employers to take on only persons who are recognised by some accepted standards of training as being properly qualified for the job.

Moreover there are certain professional skills where the 'employer' (for example, the citizen in ill-health or in conflict with the law) needs the services of a professional person (for example, a doctor or a lawyer) who is highly trained in techniques which the 'employer' does not begin to understand. Some system for an independent determination of the necessary skills and for an independent judgement on who has and who has not acquired those skills is desirable in cases of this kind. But even doctors and lawyers are human and will wish to maintain their earnings by restricting entry to their profession. Neither the closed guilds of the professionals nor the closed unions of other workers must be allowed to decide for themselves what the needed qualifications are. This is a task for independent bodies composed of uninterested outsiders set up to assess and pass judgement upon the information and advice given to them by the members of the professional organisation or trade union concerned.

In general the intelligent radical will recognise that the prohibition of unnecessary restrictive practices by industrial or professional workers is as desirable as the prohibition of unnecessary restrictive practices by producers, to which reference has already been made (see page 49 above). Much progress has been made through the Monopolies Commission and the Restrictive Practices legislation to control restrictions by producers. The intelligent radical will support the institution of similar controls over restrictive practices by workers.

There remains one question of great importance. The intelligent radical will appreciate the importance of social arrangements which encourage the participation of citizens in the day-to-day decisions which affect their lives. How far are the institutional arrangements proposed in this Chapter compatible with workers' participation in the decisions which affect their conditions of work but which are taken by the concerns which employ them?

This problem, like so many others, would be relatively easy to solve if only it were possible to avoid large-scale organisations. Consider the ultimate, final form of workers' participation, namely the situation in which the workers themselves own and manage the productive concern. They hire the capital employed at the market rate of interest; they set up their own jointly-agreed arrangements for managing the concern; they receive no fixed wage, but share out among themselves the surplus which is left over from the sale of their output after paying for materials and other inputs and after meeting the interest on their borrowed capital.

Such an organisation will be more easily set up if the scale of production is small so that only a limited number of partner-workers are involved in reaching agreement. It will be more easily set up if the production in which it is involved is labour-intensive in the sense that the technology involved requires little capital per worker; for in this case it will be easier for the partner-workers themselves to contribute or to borrow from others the limited amount of capital necessary to launch the enterprise. Nor is that all. Where little capital per head is required the risks run by the

E

partner-workers will be smaller and the co-operative principle will, therefore, be more attractive.[1]

Small-scale labour-intensive enterprises are thus the sectors of the economy in which this extreme form of worker participation is most likely to flourish. These are also the sectors of the economy in which the advantages of full workers' participation can be enjoyed without the threat of other serious social disadvantages.

This can best be seen by considering the case of a labour-owned and labour-managed concern which, because of the economies of large scale, was necessarily a monopolistic organisation. For example, consider the possibility of turning over the railway system to the ownership and management of the railwaymen. If the workers in such a monopoly enterprise could control the employment of new workers as the existing workers retired and if the very natural objective of the remaining workers were to do the best they could for themselves and their families, they would have a powerful incentive to restrict output and the numbers employed in order to raise the price which consumers would pay for the product and so to maintain and improve their earnings per head.[2]

Labour management in large-scale monopolistic concerns thus carries with it grave dangers of restrictive action; and this is the great argument against guild-socialist or syndicalist solutions to the social problem. At the other extreme these dangers disappear entirely in the case of small-scale labour-intensive concerns. For

---

[1] Compare two lines of business, both of which employ 100 workers; but in concern I the interest on the debt incurred is £50,000 a year while in concern II it is £100,000 a year. Suppose the annual product of concern I to be selling for £150,000 a year while that of concern II is selling for £200,000 a year. In both cases the workers will be receiving in total £100,000 (i.e. £1,000 a year per head), made up in concern I of total receipts of £150,000 minus debt interest of £50,000 and in concern II of total receipts of £200,000 minus debt interest of £100,000. Suppose that both concerns face the risk of a 10 per cent fall in the selling price of the product. The workers' receipts in concern I would fall by £15,000 or 15 per cent (from £100,000 to £85,000), but the workers' receipts in concern II would fall by £20,000 or 20 per cent (from £100,000 to £80,000). The risk to the worker-partners would be greater in concern II than in concern I.

[2] A monopolistic labour-managed enterprise which aims at maximising net profit per worker will be even more restrictive than a monopolistic capitalist enterprise which aims at maximising total profit. Suppose output and employment have been restricted until total profit is at a maximum. A small further restriction will not raise total profit, but it will raise profit per worker because it will reduce the number of workers between whom the total profit must be distributed.

if in any such concern earnings per worker should rise above the level obtainable in alternative employments new groups of worker-partners would be attracted into the industry; and the entry of a new co-operative enterprise would be relatively easy both because only a small group of new workers would be concerned to organise the new concern and also because the amount of capital which each worker would have to raise would be moderate.

We have discussed participation in its most extreme form simply in order to underline the basic problem, which arises in a lesser degree in the case of other and less extreme forms of participation. It is extremely desirable to promote forms of workers' participation which do enable the men and women concerned to have a say in the details of the decisions affecting their work, their hours, their safety, and the many other relevant conditions. But if the sort of society which is advocated in this book is to have any reality such participation must not be allowed to give monopolistic, restrictive powers to groups of workers in large-scale enterprises. This consideration emphasises once more the great desirability of encouraging small-scale enterprise wherever that is possible; for in the case of small-scale enterprise the most extreme forms of workers' participation will have to operate within the framework of potential competition from newly established enterprises. But in the case of large-scale enterprises the problem is much more difficult. Any institution which is set up to extend into the labour market the prohibition of noxious restrictive practices will be faced with the unenviable task of drawing a commonsensical line between legitimate forms of participation in decision-making about conditions of work and illegitimate attempts to restrict output and employment.

The intelligent radical will regret that in this wicked world in some cases precisely defined rules must give place to common-sensical adhoccery; but he will face the facts of life and admit this to be a case in point.

V

The Distribution of Income and Property:
(1) *Indirect Measures*

The intelligent radical is at heart an incurable egalitarian and is appalled by the gross inequalities which he observes in modern society. But he desires to cope with them by methods which are compatible with the maintenance of a free and an efficient economic system.

One method which he rejects is to redistribute real income by the manipulation of relative prices, raising the prices of the things which the poor man sells and the rich man buys and lowering the prices of the things which the rich man sells and the poor man buys. This method is in any case incompatible with the principle of making prices, including wage rates, more and more responsive to conditions of supply and demand in each particular market, a principle which has been advocated in the preceding Chapters of this book. But it is useful to examine in a little more detail some examples of the far-reaching problems raised by any attempt to redistribute income through the control of relative prices.

A straightforward example of an attempt to improve the incomes of the poor by raising the price of what they sell is the attempt to guarantee a minimum income to all workers by setting a minimum wage below which it is illegal to employ a worker. This raises the following problems.

First, minimum wage legislation can do nothing to help those self-employed persons whose earnings are low.

Second, to meet its purpose of ensuring a minimum standard of life for those who are employed by others the minimum wage would have to be set in terms of minimum weekly earnings. But if this were done it would be unprofitable to employ part-time or casual workers, since to pay a full week's wage for a few hours' work would be out of the question. If, however, the minimum is set in terms of a minimum hourly wage rate, part-time work is no longer ruled out; but the person who can obtain only part-time work will not necessarily obtain an income which corresponds to the minimum which the legislation is designed to ensure.

Third, an effective minimum wage, whether it be on the basis of the hourly wage or of weekly earnings, may deprive some persons of the possibility of obtaining employment. There are sectors of the labour market for relatively unskilled work – particularly for older workers, for workers in depressed occupations, industries, or localities, and for disabled workers – where the value of the output of the worker is low and where, therefore, employment opportunities will depend upon the wage payment being low. This does not imply that nothing should be done to push up low wages where low wages are due to the monopsonistic exploitation of the workers. Nor, of course, does it mean that nothing should be done to bring industry to depressed areas, to subsidise employment in such areas, to retrain labour, to enable workers to move to regions and occupations where prospects are better. But it does imply that when all is said and done there will remain cases in which certain persons can only do work which though it is useful is of low value; and in such cases it is much better to allow such persons to find employment at a low wage (with their earnings supplemented from other sources as we will later suggest on pages 89–92 below) than it is to insist upon a wage in excess of the value of their output, which will drive them into unemployment (in which case the whole of their income must come from other sources).

Fourth, there are serious difficulties in evaluating the true value of the wage where, as in the case of domestic service, a large part of the wage takes the form of a payment in kind.

Fifth, the interpretation and enforcement of the minimum wage raise serious administrative problems with yet one more apparatus of bureaucratic control.

A good example of attempts to improve the distribution of real income by holding down the price of something which the poor man buys from the rich man is legislation to control rents of dwelling houses and to keep them below what the market rent would otherwise be. But this policy also raises a number of very awkward problems.

First, by no means all landlords are rich and all tenants poor. A house may be owned and let by an otherwise impoverished widow and quite rich people may rent a dwelling house or apartment.

Second, an attempt may be made to restrict the privilege of low rents to those who are less well off by ruling that the restriction of rent applies only to dwellings which are likely to be inhabited by the poor. Rent control would thus not be applied to office buildings or to dwellings which were likely to be inhabited by the wealthy (e.g. dwellings with a rateable value above a certain figure). But any such rule would give a great incentive to builders to concentrate their building efforts on office accommodation, expensive houses whose rents would be uncontrolled, or houses for owner-occupation which the poor would be less likely than the rich to be able to finance. Thus new resources would be siphoned off to satisfy the needs of the rich rather than the poor.

Third, there would be no incentive on the part of private landlords of rent-controlled dwellings to improve those dwellings or even to keep them in good repair if the return on such investment was kept below the market level.

Fourth, in order to offset the lack of private incentive to build, improve, and repair dwellings for letting to persons other than the rich, the public authorities – either the central government or the local authorities or both – would have to become more and more involved in ensuring that such dwellings were kept in good repair and in providing new dwellings themselves.

Fifth, rent control must be combined with regulations which give tenants security of tenure of their tenancy of the dwellings in which they live. Otherwise the private landlord would be free to eject the tenant and sell the dwelling on which the rent return was inadequate to some other family which was wealthy enough to be able to purchase the dwelling for owner occupation. But such security of tenure will lead to a waste of accommodation. Consider a man and woman bringing up a family in a dwelling of a suitable size. The children marry and leave home. The ageing parents are left in the family house with more rooms than they need. But they may well be unwilling to move from the existing five-room family house to a small two-room apartment suitable for an ageing couple because they have security of tenure of the existing house at a very low rent and find it difficult or impossible to find cheaper alternative accommodation.

Sixth, for exactly similar reasons rent control is likely to impede the mobility of labour from one region to another in response to economic changes which make new occupations in new localities more useful and more rewarding than existing ones. A worker may be unwilling to lose security of tenure of an existing dwelling at a low rent in his old region to take a higher paid post in a new region where he has no such dwelling to occupy.

Seventh, the disincentive to the building of new dwellings to let and the waste of existing accommodation, which we have already discussed, are likely to lead to an excess of demand over the supply of dwellings to let. Indeed, an excess of demand over supply is the natural outcome of a state of affairs in which a price is kept below its market level. This means that many persons – and in particular many newly married couples setting up house for the first time – who are not in the privileged group of existing tenants with security of tenure of exceptionally low-rented dwellings will be homeless and unable to find any suitable dwelling.

Eighth, the enforcement of rent controls, the need to ensure that private dwellings are kept in decent repair, and the necessity for the public authorities to shoulder ever-increasing responsibility to supply new dwellings and to provide for the homeless – all these things will necessitate one more elaborate set of bureaucratic controls and regulations.

The same sort of difficulties arise when local authorities keep the level of the rents which they charge on council houses far below the market level of rents. Demand once more will exceed supply. Some of the unlucky outsiders, low on the waiting list for the privilege of an exceptionally low-rented council house, may be low-paid workers, while many of the historically lucky persons who have already entered the charmed circle of good housing at exceptionally low rents may be highly-paid. Accommodation may be wasted and mobility impeded because, as in the case of private tenancies, the security of tenure which must go with the restriction of rents below market values removes the incentive to seek other more appropriate accommodation.

A similar mistaken policy in the housing market is the exemption of owner-occupiers from taxation on the annual value of their houses. By no means all owner-occupiers are poor. Consider rich Mr A using stock exchange dividends to rent a house from rich Mr B. Mr A will pay income tax at a high rate on his investment income and will pay rent to Mr B out of the remainder of his tax-free income. Mr B will then pay income tax at a high rate on the rent received from Mr A. This is as it should be; there are two rich men and two incomes from two important real capital assets, one from the profits of the companies whose shares are owned by Mr A, and one from the annual value of the house owned by Mr B. If now Mr A hands over his shares to Mr B and Mr B hands over the house to Mr A so that Mr A is now an owner-occupier, according to present arrangements no tax will be paid on the annual value of the house, though tax will, of course, still be payable on the investment income.

The undesirable results of this are fourfold : first, it is a way of giving tax exemption on a most important part of the real income of owner-occupiers provided they are rich enough to pay

tax, an exemption which is the more important the richer the
man concerned and the higher the rate of tax to which he is
liable; second, it encourages the demand for housing by the rich,
since this form of investment has so important a tax privilege,
and thus diverts building resources and available land to the rich
end of the market and drives up the price of houses and building
land against the poorer end of the market; third, it greatly dis-
courages the building of houses for letting as contrasted with
building for owner-occupiers, although for many poorer families
renting a dwelling is more feasible than purchasing a dwelling;
and, fourth, by reducing in an important way the tax base, it
means that the rates of taxation on the remaining sources of
income must be so much the higher in order to raise the total
tax revenue which is needed on other budgetary grounds.

The intelligent radical will regard the market for housing as
an outstanding case in which the sensible method of combining
efficiency, freedom, and equity is to allow the rents of dwellings,
whether provided by private or by public landlords, to move
much more towards their free-market levels, to equalise the
taxation as between rented and owner-occupied dwellings, and
to subsidise in a more direct fashion (as discussed later in Chapter
VI) the incomes of the poor at the expense of the incomes of the
rich.

The intelligent radical will recognise, however, that there are
special cases in which this set of general principles cannot be
appropriately applied and where on distributional grounds the
provision of certain essential goods or services at a low or zero
price may be the best arrangement.

The National Health Service is a case in point. Consider the
application to the problems of health of the general principle
of taking direct fiscal measures to redistribute incomes and of
then allowing individuals to purchase their own goods in the
market. In the case of medical services this would mean allowing
individuals, after an appropriate direct redistribution of incomes,
to insure privately against the medical costs which they would
incur if they were ill.

But this solution would be subject to the following special conditions :

(1) Some persons are less healthy than others. Those whose
medical prospects are bad would have to pay higher insurance
premiums than those whose prospects are good. An equitable distribution of incomes would, therefore, have to allow more for
the needs of the unhealthy than for the needs of the healthy.

This would require advance medical investigation by the medical profession in order to inform properly the insurance companies and the government authorities about the health risks of different individuals, so that suitable differentials in insurance premiums and in public support of incomes could be established.

(2) Insurance would probably have to be compulsory, since society will hardly care to leave untreated medically those persons who became ill, having failed to insure and being unable to pay for their treatment out of other resources. But if free medicine were provided for the improvident, the incentive to insure would be removed.

(3) When persons became ill, it would be for the doctor and not for the patient to certify to the insurance company that such-and-such a medical expense was justified.

The state of affairs is thus one in which (1) on distributional grounds the State has to support persons according to their medical needs rather than merely to redistribute incomes more equally; (2) such financial support as the individual receives on these grounds must be compulsorily paid over to medical insurance funds; and (3) the doctors who actually provide the medical service must themselves also judge whether expenditure out of such funds is medically justifiable or not. In such circumstances it would be more straightforward for the State to provide out of general taxation free medical service to those whom the doctors themselves decide to need the service.[1]

In general, however, the intelligent radical will advocate more direct general measures for the redistribution of income and property in preference to particular interventions in particular markets for this purpose. What form should such general measures take? In order to answer this question it is useful to consider what are the features of modern societies which give rise to gross economic inequalities.

Some such inequalities can be explained by the maintenance of privileged positions through artificial professional or trade union restrictions which prevent one citizen, although he is in fact well qualified, from entering into a protected well-paid occu-

[1] There remain, of course, immensely difficult economic problems in the administration of a free Health Service. Resources for such a service must be limited. To what level should they be limited? Within those limits what are the priorities — to save a few lives by highly expensive, technologically sophisticated operations and equipment? to add to the comforts of those in geriatric wards? to attack the common cold? And who other than the doctors should decide? To consider these problems is beyond the scope of this short book.

pation. An extreme example of this is where some persons remain unemployed because the high real wage rates which are maintained for those in work remove the incentive to give employment to the whole working force.

But inequalities of this kind would themselves be removed by the adoption of the policies for full employment and for free and easy movement between occupations, which have been proposed in the preceding Chapters. There is no conflict between the restoration of the price-market mechanism and the promotion of real equality of opportunity. The more fully the proposals made in Chapters II, III, and IV are implemented, the more nearly will it be true that those citizens who are equally well endowed with income-earning capacities will enjoy equal opportunities for exploiting those capacities.

But not all citizens are equally well endowed. Some persons are born with innate qualities of physique, of intellect, or of personality which enable them to earn more than others. Some persons have received an education and training which enables them to succeed better than others. Some persons have family, school, and university backgrounds which enable them to make social contacts which will prove more useful to them in their subsequent careers than the social backgrounds of others. Some persons inherit much more income-bearing property from their parents than do others. Initial endowments of genes, education, social contacts, and property differ greatly from individual to individual.

Moreover these endowments of fortune feed upon each other. A man with high innate ability may be able to earn a large income from which he can save and accumulate property. His high income and wealth will enable him to move in circles of society where he can make useful contacts with others who can help him in his opportunities for obtaining even more rewarding jobs and even more profitable investments. As he becomes rich he can afford to consult stock brokers and others who may enable him to obtain by capital gains as well as investment income a higher yield on his large property than the poor man can on his small savings; and the exceptionally high rate of return on his exceptionally high property will lead to a very high income from property, from which he can save still further sums to accumulate a still larger capital. At the other extreme a citizen without good initial endowments may find it difficult to earn enough to leave any margin to start accumulating any capital; he will find it less easy to make social contacts which will help him to find better jobs; the yield on any small savings which he does make may be relatively low.

There are in society many of these positive feedbacks, of this principle of 'to-him-that-hath-shall-be-given' and of 'from-him-that-hath-not-shall-be-taken'. Good and bad endowments of fortune are likely to reinforce each other, so that the rich become richer and the poor poorer. The resulting good or bad fortunes can then be handed down from one generation to another. Good genetic ability, good social contacts, and large properties can be handed down from parents to their children; and rich parents can afford to give exceptional schooling and training to their children.

But at the same time there are some forces in society working in the opposite direction and setting limits to the resulting inequalities of income and property. Rich men do not need to earn or to accumulate property as much as poor men; and the rich may, therefore, tend to spend all their income and to retire from earning income. In so far as they do this, they set limits to the further expansion of their incomes and properties. But much more important are the policies adopted by the government to interrupt the disequalising processes of society. Free health and educational services for all citizens; family allowances; unemployment, health and sickness benefits; old-age pensions; progressive taxation of income and wealth : all these policies tend towards the negative feedback principles of 'from-him-that-hath-shall-be-taken' and 'to-him-that-hath-not-shall-be-given'. It is on policies of this kind that the intelligent radical will lay the greatest stress and we will discuss them at length in the next Chapter.

There is, however, one other very important equalising influence. In so far as men in the choice of their wives or women in the choice of their husbands select mates whose fortunes differ from their own, there will be an equalising factor at work. If the most fortunate man always married the most fortunate woman, the second most fortunate man always married the second most fortunate woman, and so on down the list, marriage and inheritance would exert no equalising influence. But in so far as a rich man marries a poor woman, or a poor man marries a rich woman, the large and the small properties will be averaged before being passed on to the next generation. This principle is true of all the endowments of good or bad fortune – genetic ability, educational background, social contacts, and property. In so far as the fortunate marry the less fortunate, the fortunes inherited by the next generation will tend to be equalised. In fact mating is very assortative in present society, in the sense that the fortunate tend to marry the fortunate and the unfortunate to marry the unfortunate. But marriage is not perfectly assortative; and every time two persons of different fortunes marry, the fortunes inherited by the children will be *pro tanto* averaged and equalised.

So far no mention has been made of pure luck in life, a phenomenon which is a powerful disequalising force. Two men with the same initial endowments of fortune and with similar characters may fare very differently in life because one happens to choose an occupation which flourishes, to invest his money in a successful enterprise, and to meet someone who gives him a good chance in his career, while the other man may happen to choose an occupation in an industry which declines, to invest his money in an enterprise which goes bankrupt, and to meet congenial, but otherwise unrewarding companions. It is the man who, like Henry Ford, combines ability with the luck of having the right idea at the right time in the right place whose economic wealth may explode, while an equally able man with less luck may plod through life. Good or bad luck can introduce great inequalities even as between persons who start with equally good or bad initial endowments of fortune.

One can best look upon the forces in society which determine the ultimate degree of inequality in the distribution of income and wealth in the following way.

(1) There are continuous random strokes of luck causing some persons to prosper and others to stagnate. Luck is thus one of the basic forces continually reintroducing inequalities.

(2) There are many structural, self-reinforcing influences at work which maintain and emphasise any inequalities that happen to exist. Initial good or bad endowments of ability, education, social contacts, and property tend to reinforce each other and be handed down in a family from one generation to another.

(3) These disequalising forces of luck and of structural relationships which reinforce and magnify the influences of good or of bad fortune are in part mitigated and offset by other forces and, in particular, by governmental measures for redistribution from rich to poor.

(4) Inequalities are in large measure handed down by inheritance from generation to generation; but in so far as marriage causes any averaging of fortunes, it represents an equalising factor, the strength of which depends upon the degree to which the fortunate marry the less fortunate.

Thus luck and the self-reinforcing structures of good or bad fortune in society (elements 1 and 2 above) are always reintroducing and emphasising inequalities, while governmental offsetting policies and inter-marriage are reducing inequalities (elements 3 and 4 above). The outcome differs from society to society according to the force of these conflicting influences.

This analysis of inequalities suggests that there are two basically different ways of attempting to reduce inequalities of income and wealth.

The first method is to alter the social and economic structural relationships in society in such a way that citizens not only have equality of opportunity, but also start in life with much more equal initial endowments of fortune. In this case – apart from the influence of pure luck – one might expect a much more equal outcome of income and property.

The second basic type of policy is to tackle the problem of inequality directly by redistributive fiscal measures, taxing whatever riches and subsidising whatever poverty, luck and the structure of society may occasion.

The intelligent radical will put great stress on these direct fiscal measures for the redistribution of income and wealth. In the first place, the restructuring of social relationships is bound to be a long drawn out affair and its indirect effects upon equality will only be gradually felt as the generations succeed each other. Second, strokes of good and bad luck will continue and will remain extremely important in reintroducing inequalities, however much the basic structure of social relationships is reformed. Third, direct fiscal measures for the redistribution of income and wealth will themselves help to change the basic structure of social relationships, since a direct redistribution of wealth in one generation will mean that the next generation starts with less inequality in its inherited endowments.

But while for the attainment of any appreciable immediate effect priority must be given to direct fiscal measures of redistribution, the intelligent radical will not wish to overlook the longer-term structural reforms which may help to equalise the inheritance of initial endowments of good and bad fortune. Accordingly we will devote the rest of this Chapter to some discussion of such structural reforms; and in the following Chapter we will consider the design of efficient and fair fiscal measures for the direct redistribution of incomes and properties.

Differences in the amount and quality of the education and training which different citizens have received can account for considerable differences in subsequent earning power. The question therefore arises whether steps could be taken so to develop the educational system as to equalise initial educational endowments. There can be little doubt that in the past the extension of free primary education by the State to all children has been an important equalising influence. Every citizen has had such resources invested in his basic education, without which the children of the poor might have remained illiterate and even more disadvantaged than they are at present relatively to the children of the rich. At the next stage of education there are also important equalising influences. The expansion of training which turns unskilled into skilled workers may be calculated to reduce the supply of the former and to increase the supply of the latter type of worker thus tending to raise the wages of the unskilled relatively to the skilled. Such equalisation of earnings and closing of differentials (for example, as between clerical workers and manual workers) has in fact occurred over the last decades.

A similar equalising tendency may be expected from certain developments in university education. The expansion in volume of such education may be expected to have an equalising effect in so far as it also represents a process of upgrading more young men and women from grades of lower skill to grades of higher skill, thus reducing the supply of lower paid and increasing the supply of higher paid workers.

But in the case of higher education this is not the whole of the story. University education, unlike the earlier stages of education, is bound to remain selective; not every young man and woman would gain from such higher training. In so far as selection for state financed university education is made more and more on the merits of the candidates themselves rather than on the wealth or social position of their parents, the position is reached at which larger and larger investment in higher training is concentrated more and more exclusively on those members of society who are in any case innately well endowed with ability. This is to emphasise the principle of 'to-him-that-hath-shall-be-given'.

There are many desirable forms of educational development which will have further important equalising effects. An outstanding example is to improve the quality of primary education in deprived areas where educational and other social services are themselves of inferior quality. But the intelligent radical will not close his eyes to the fact that in some instances the best use of further funds for the development of the educational system may well raise the familiar conflict between the social objectives of efficiency and of equality. In order to raise economic productivity one would want to concentrate the investment of funds for further training in the ways which would most promote the productivity of those who are trained; and in many cases this may mean giving an expensive technical training to the most able members of the community who are best able to gain from such training. But to promote equality one would need to concentrate resources on the dullards and to leave the bright boys and girls relatively untrained, in the hope that the greater training of the dullards might compensate for the better innate capacity of the bright young men and women.

There is another closely related problem which is raised by the expansion of higher education and the selection for it of the ablest young men and women from all classes in society. This is one important way of promoting social mobility and of increasing equality of opportunity by opening all careers to the talented from all classes. Such measures which break down rigid social barriers between members of different social classes and which increase equality of opportunity will be greatly welcomed by the intelligent radical. He will do so because he values equality of opportunity in and for itself.

But the ultimate effects on economic inequalities are less certain. On the one hand the mixture of bright young men and women from all classes in the university is likely to lead to less assortative mating in so far as the inheritance of property and social contacts are concerned. A young man or woman from a propertied and socially well-connected family is more likely than before to choose a marriage partner from a less wealthy and less well connected family. The averaging of good and bad fortunes over the generations may thus be increased.

But as far as innate ability is concerned the development of higher education may increase the degree of assortative mating. If all the able boys and girls are gathered together regardless of class, they are likely to inter-marry; and in consequence there may grow up a meritocratic élite in which ability, earning power, and hence the ability to accumulate property become more and more concentrated.

The intelligent radical will recognise that an efficient development of higher education may in some cases require the concentration of educational investment on those who are already endowed with exceptional innate capacity and that it may also lead to an even greater assortative mating between the ablest members of society. He will not conclude from this that the whole purpose of higher education should be shifted from the training of the bright to the training of the dull; but he will recognise that it greatly increases the case for direct fiscal measures to redistribute any resulting inequalities of income and wealth.[1]

Demographic changes in fertility can also have a long-term structural effect upon inequalities in endowments. In recent years the well-to-do have had greater knowledge of contraceptive methods, easier access to contraceptive services, and greater ability to afford effective contraceptive devices. Family limitations thus started among the fortunate members of society, so that in recent years the family size of the rich has been smaller than the family size of the poor.

If this continued, it would in the long run have a serious effect in causing a still greater concentration of wealth on those families which are already well to do. There are three reasons why if the rich have smaller families than the poor, inequalities in income and wealth are likely to be increased.

First, there is the obvious point that children need to be fed, clothed, housed, and generally supported. They cost money. If the ratio of dependent children to income-earning parents is higher among the poor than among the rich inequalities in income per head (including the heads of the dependent children) will be *pro tanto* increased.

Second, the very fact that there are many children to support will make it more difficult for the poor families to save, and the fact that there are few children to support will make it easier for the rich families to save. Capital accumulation will proceed at a still more unequal rate as between rich and poor families.

Third, not only do large families make it more difficult for the parents to save and so to acquire property, but they also mean that when the parents die whatever property they have managed to acquire must be split up into many small fragments to be bequeathed to the large number of sons and daughters. If the family is small, then the parent's property on their death can be concentrated on the few surviving children. Many heirs in poor

[1] In particular he will recognise that there is a case for the finance of higher education in part by the grant of loans to students, repayable out of their future earnings if they are successful in their subsequent careers. Where Tom has thousands of pounds invested by the State in his higher education because he is a bright lad, while Dick has to go out to work at once in a less well-paid occupation because he is not so bright, it is not unfair or improper that Tom should later be asked to repay part of the cost of his training.

families and few heirs in rich families will, as each generation succeeds the preceding generation, continuously accentuate inequalities in inherited property.

Social-demographic changes which reduce the fertility of the unfortunate relatively to the fertility of the fortunate families will, therefore, help towards the equalisation of economic wealth. They have the immediate effect of reducing the costs to the poor, relatively to the costs to the rich, of bringing up children; and they have the longer-run effects of reducing the difficulty for the poor relatively to the rich of acquiring some property and of causing inherited property to be less fragmented among the children of the poor relatively to those of the rich.

The intelligent radical will realise that the very success of the policies which he advocates for increasing social mobility and for equalising opportunities for all citizens will reinforce the case for ensuring that the less fortunate members of society have ready access to the knowledge and means necessary to enable them to limit the size of their families. The greater the degree of social mobility and of equality of access to economic opportunities, the more probable the movement of the innately able upwards, and of the innately less well endowed downwards, on the ladder of economic prosperity; and any such tendency for the concentration of innate abilities would be even more marked if the breakdown of social privilege in education encouraged assortative mating according to innate ability rather than according to social and economic privilege. In these conditions it would become more and more probable that a somewhat higher family size among the fortunate than among the unfortunate would lead to some improvement in the average level of innate ability in society.[1]

But to return to the problem of inequalities, more heirs for the rich and fewer heirs for the poor might in the long run have an appreciable effect upon the distribution of property. But that would be a very long drawn out effect. If anything significant is to be done here and now about the equalisation of initial endowments in property rights, it is clear that more direct and dramatic measures must be taken by the government to affect

[1] This is not, however, a development which is likely to reduce inequalities. To reduce inequalities of genetic factors for ability one would need to reduce the fertility of the very able and the very dull and to raise the fertility of the mediocre. Any measures which had the effect of increasing the reproduction of high innate ability and reducing the reproduction of low innate ability might be expected to raise average ability but not to equalise abilities. But the intelligent radical will be interested in raising the average as well as in reducing inequalities.

F

the inheritance of property. This implies a radical change in the tax treatment of wealth and of its inheritance; and this makes up an important part of the redesign of our general fiscal arrangements for the redistribution of income and property, which constitutes the subject matter of the following Chapter.

VI

The Distribution of Income and Property:
(2)   *Fiscal Measures*

One of the most marked features of our present society is the very
unequal distribution of the ownership of property. Inequalities
in earnings are very great, but inequalities in the ownership of
properties are much greater still. The intelligent radical has no
desire to put an end to private property, since he values the
independence of action and the decentralisation of power that
can be achieved through a wide spread of the individual ownership of private property. But he does strongly object to the existing
excessive inequalities of private property and to the large concentrations of power and privilege which they involve. His ideal
society is a property-owning democracy in which every able-
bodied citizen is both a worker and a property-owner and in
which the existing inequalities both in income and in property
are greatly moderated.

Death duties afford one of the most obvious weapons for remov-
ing and avoiding over the years excessive accumulations of
inherited wealth. But in order that any system of death duties
should be effective two major loop-holes for the avoidance of such
duties have first to be closed.

The first obvious method of avoiding death duties is for the
parent before he dies to give away to his children or other
potential heirs a large part of his property, leaving only a small
amount in his own possession to be taxed at his death. Some system
of taxing gifts between the living must be incorporated into any
tax system which is designed to make duties on inherited property
really effective.

The second main method of avoiding death duties is through
the use of trusts. A trust enables a distinction to be made between
the legal owners of a property (the trustees) and those who will in
fact benefit from the property. Thus Grandpa Smith dies leaving
his property to trustees (Cousin Tom and Cousin Harry) under
a trust deed which enables Cousins Tom and Harry to use the
income from the property at their discretion to the benefit of any
descendants of Grandpa Smith. Cousins Tom and Harry first

use the trust funds for the benefit of Grandpa Smith's son whom we will call Father Smith and when Father Smith dies they use the funds for the benefit of Father Smith's son whom we will call Son Smith, and so on. Thus the beneficial use of the property has passed twice, first from Grandpa Smith to Father Smith and second from Father Smith to Son Smith but its legal ownership has passed only once on Grandpa Smith's death to Cousins Tom and Harry. Unless special measures are taken this inherited wealth will have been taxed only once instead of twice.

The above is only one of the simplest and most obvious ways in which the distinction made possible by the institution of a trust between the legal and the beneficial ownership of a property can be used to avoid tax. Tax lawyers are ingenious people and the possibilities are clearly manifold. The intelligent radical will favour a truly radical solution to this problem, namely the elimination or very severe limitation of the use of trusts. What is needed is that on his death or on giving away his property during his life each owner of property should bequeath or give his property to certain precise and clearly defined existing individuals as beneficial owners of the property. This is not incompatible with Grandpa Smith leaving a life interest in his property to Father Smith with reversion of ownership on Father Smith's death to some other named person, such as Son Smith if Son Smith already exists. The present value of Father Smith's life interest and of Son Smith's expectation of the reversion can be assessed; the whole property will have been left in fact to two clearly-defined persons. What must be ruled out is the power to obscure the future beneficial ownership of the property. In his clear-cut approach to this issue the intelligent radical will be fortified in his views by the thought that the trust is a peculiar invention of English law and that foreigners get on very well with the simple idea that each bit of private property should at any given time be clearly owned by some precise beneficial owner.

Once it is ruled that gifts between the living should be treated for tax like gifts from the dead to the living and that every kind of gift should be a gift to some precisely defined existing beneficiary it becomes possible to design a system of duties on the transfer of wealth which will have the greatest effect on evening out the ownership of inherited property. Such a tax, known as the accessions duty, is levied on the following principle.

A record is kept of the total amount of property which any given citizen, Mr Smith, has received by way of gift or inheritance over the whole of his life up to date. The person who gave or left the property to Mr Smith is not taxed. But Mr Smith is taxed at a progressive rate on the total amount of property which he has thus acquired. That is to say, on the first £5,000 he might pay no tax, on the second £5,000 of his total acquisition to date – a sum which he might have received from a quite different benefactor at a subsequent date – he might pay 10 per cent in tax, and so on up a progressive scale.

Such a tax would give the maximum incentive to a wealthy citizen to dispose of his property by spreading it widely among beneficiaries who have themselves not yet received any substantial inheritances. At the extreme a millionaire would avoid all duty on his estate if he split it up in many small bequests each of which went to someone who had not yet acquired any property from anyone else by way of gift or inheritance.

There is one further provision that could very usefully be introduced into such a system of taxation. The rate of duty which would be payable on any given gift or bequest to Mr Smith from Mr Jones might be made to depend not only upon the total amount of property which Mr Smith had already acquired by gift of inheritance, but also upon the difference in age between Mr Smith and Mr Jones. The greater the excess of the age of the donor over the age of the recipient, the higher would be the rate of duty.

The underlying reason for this proposal is clear. If Mr Smith receives £10,000 when he is twenty years old, it is clearly worth more to him than if he receives it when he is eighty years old; he is likely to have many more years in which to enjoy its income. If Mr Jones gives his property away when he is twenty years old instead of waiting until he is eighty years old, he would clearly have had less years in which to enjoy its income. Thus a bequest from an old man to a young man should properly bear a greater tax burden than a bequest from a young man to an old man. Or, to put the same point another way, the older the givers and the younger the recipients, the smaller the number of times that a property will pass from one owner to another in a century; and the more appropriate, therefore, is it to levy a higher rate of tax on the rare occasions when it does become taxable.

It may be helpful to illustrate this general principle by two particular examples.

The first example is that of the introduction of generation skipping in the inheritance of a family property. Suppose that Grandpa Smith leaves his money to Father Smith who then leaves his money to Son Smith; the bequests are taxed twice. Suppose instead that Grandpa Smith leaves his money direct to Son Smith; the bequest pays duty only once. But since the age difference between Grandpa Smith and Son Smith will be much greater than the age difference between Grandpa Smith and Father Smith or the age difference between Father Smith and Son Smith, the incentive to Grandpa Smith to skip a generation will be much reduced by the fact that the rate of tax will be higher. The property will bear tax once at a high rate instead of twice at a low rate.[1]

The second example is that of gifts between husband and wife. The accessions tax must be based upon individual ownership of wealth. It would be administratively very difficult and in fact probably undesirable in any case to treat the joint property of husband and wife as if it were in single ownership. Yet one will not want to be severe in taxation on gifts beween husband and wife which equalise their properties. The age-difference provision helps to meet this point. Since the difference in age between husband and wife will be much less than that between parent and child, the taxation on such transfers between spouses will be much moderated.[2]

---

[1] The ultimate effect of a continuing process of generation skipping is a loss of revenue not because properties change hands less frequently but because at each change of ownership a smaller property is transferred. Consider case I of a family fortune of £100 passing from father to son in a family in which each father has a son at the age of thirty and lives on till the age of seventy, leaving the family fortune of £100 to his son who will then be aged forty. At any one time there will be a single family fortune of £100 owned by a member of the family between the age of forty (at which he inherited) and the age of seventy (at which he dies). The family fortune of £100 will change hands once every thirty years between a father aged seventy and a son aged forty. Contrast this with case II of a family with a total fortune of £100 but in which each male member at the age of ten receives an inheritance of £50 from his grandfather who died at the age of seventy; this child's father will then be forty years old, having already held for thirty years a fortune of £50 which he inherited when he was ten from his grandfather. In this case the total family fortune of £100 will be split into two individual fortunes of £50. At any one time one of these will be held by a man between the ages of forty and seventy (having been received when the holder was ten) and the other by his son between the ages of ten and forty. There will thus be two fortunes of £50 each, each changing hands once every 60 years. Thus in case I one fortune of £100 will change hands every thirtieth year and in case II one fortune of £50 will change hands every thirtieth year. The amount of tax paid would be lower in case II than in case I unless a supplementary tax was paid because of the greater disparity of age between benefactor and beneficiary.

[2] It is to be noted that the age-difference provision does not discourage parents from giving property to their young children during their life-

So much for fiscal reform to encourage a structural redistribution of inherited property. If the rate of tax on successive acquisitions rose at a sufficiently steep progression after a certain amount of property had been acquired, it would become virtually impossible for any citizen in the future to receive by gift or inheritance more than a strictly limited total fortune. But the results of such a reform would take time to work themselves out. Moreover, differences in the inheritance of property are, as we have seen, not the only causes of differences of income and wealth, which depend also upon differences of ability, social contacts, and luck. More direct and immediate measures are also needed to obtain and to maintain a less unequal distribution of current purchasing power.

There are, of course, already a number of governmental measures designed for this purpose of direct redistribution. But these at present make up a terrible jumble of different *ad hoc* measures which achieves much less effective and intelligible results than could be achieved by a properly designed coherent system instituted for this express purpose.

Consider the present muddle. There are social security benefits for citizens who are unemployed or sick and state pensions for the old, some being at the same money rate for all and some being graduated according to the citizen's previous earnings. There are family allowances payable to all parents for all children except for the first child in the family. Some of these social benefits are treated as taxable for income tax purposes and some are tax free, regardless of the size of the citizen's other income. But these various social benefits are not paid on a sufficient scale to prevent the citizen who has no other income from falling into poverty. There is, therefore, a system of supplementary benefits under which any citizen can apply for further aid and will receive it if, after a means test, further aid is needed to bring him and his family above a defined poverty level – provided always that he is not in work. If he is in work, he cannot receive supplementary benefit, so that the family of a worker with a low wage and a large number of children will continue in poverty. To mitigate,

time. Such a discouragement would be given if the height of the tax depended solely on the age of the recipient and not at all upon the age of the donor; but it does not occur if the height of the tax depends upon the difference between the age of donor and of recipient. It is also worth noting that the above proposals will encourage equality as between the sexes in the ownership of property. The husband can give property to his wife (if she is in the same age group) with a minimal rate of tax, and vice versa.

but not completely to remove, this cause of poverty there is a separate system of family income supplementation whereby, under a different means-test system, some part of the deficient income of a worker with a low wage but a large family can be made good by supplementary aid, if the worker applies to be tested for this aid. In addition there is a host of other particular aids and reliefs operated under various differing tests of means by various different local and central authorities, covering remissions of rents, remissions of rates, remission of charges under the National Health Service, free provision of school meals, aid to parents with the finance of their children's further education, and so on. Finally, there is the general system of income taxation, under which the first slice of a citizen's income – depending upon the size of his family and other criteria – is allowed free of tax, and under which the rate of tax is progressively raised on the higher incomes.

The result of this mixed bag of measures is an extraordinary inflated administrative muddle with overlapping and unco-ordinated results. The total system often appears quite unintelligible to the ordinary citizen who has, for example, sometimes found himself in a position in which he is simultaneously deemed poor enough to receive family income supplementation but rich enough to pay income tax. Moreover the various means tests may so interact as to remove all incentive to earn more. Thus a worker with a large family who manages to increase his earnings may find that he is practically no better off – indeed, in the extreme case he may actually be worse off – as a result of losing various means-tested aids; he may lose 50 per cent of the increased earnings in reduced family income supplementation, he may pay 30 per cent of the increased earnings in income tax, and the remaining 20 per cent may be swallowed up in the withdrawal of other means-tested aids and remissions.

And in spite of all this, poverty still continues partly because there are still some loop-holes left in this jumble of provisions, partly because of some citizens' ignorance of their rights and of the procedures for obtaining their rights in this complex maze of official forms and rules, and partly because of personal pride which makes people unwilling to submit themselves to the various tests of means.

The intelligent radical would like to see a clean sweep to all this. Let every citizen in the country receive automatically each week a social dividend equal to the present supplementary benefit scale. This scale depends upon the composition and size of the family and is designed by parliament to represent the amount of income which must be received by a family of a given composition to keep that family out of poverty and to give it a decent standard of living. Let this social dividend be exempt from all income tax. Scrap all the other social benefits – unemployment benefit, sickness benefit, old-age pensions, family allowances – and remove all the personal allowances under the income tax, since these would be replaced by the tax-exempt social dividends.

Such a scheme would eliminate poverty in the sense that no one would be below a level set by the scale for the social dividend. It would in fact involve a marked redistribution of income, first, from the rich to the poor and, second, from the childless to those with many children. This second type of redistribution is inevitable if it is really desired to eliminate poverty and to equalise standards. Dependent children have needs but earn no income; and for this reason redistribution in favour of the families with children is an inevitable feature of any redistribution designed to adjust resources to need. This aspect of the proposal raises issues to which we will return later (see pages 120–122 below).

The scheme thus involves extensive redistribution which would effectively eliminate poverty; but – and that is the other side of the coin – it is, of course, costly. The extent of the redistribution and its cost would naturally depend upon the system of taxation employed to raise the revenue needed to finance the universal payment of the social dividends.

Solely as a means of simplifying the discussion of the relevant tax problems let us start by considering a very simple tax arrangement and then introduce into it a number of desirable modifications. Suppose, then, that all contributions to national insurance were abolished, that the differentiation between the taxation of earned and unearned incomes was eliminated, that all progression in the rates of taxation of income was removed, and that a single standard rate of tax was imposed on all personal incomes (other than the social dividend itself) at a rate sufficient to finance the social dividends and in addition to preserve the existing balance between total government revenue and expenditure, on the assumption that all other governmental taxes and expenditures remained unchanged. This arrangement would involve the standard rate of income tax being raised to 50 per cent or even somewhat more.

There are, however, at least four important desirable modifications of the above simple tax scheme which would enable this high standard rate of income tax to be reduced, namely, (1) the continued raising of revenue from graduated national insurance contributions, (2) some progressive rise in the rate of tax on the higher incomes,(3) some supplementary taxation of wealth or of unearned income, and (4) extension of the tax base by the removal of a number of existing exemptions and remissions of taxation.

The general philosophy behind points (1) and (2) above can be expressed diagrammatically in the following way. On the Figure on page 91 we measure along the horizontal axis the income which a family of a given composition receives from its earnings or interest or other sources before tax and before receipt of social dividend. Up the vertical axis we measure the income which it retains after receiving the social dividend and after paying any tax which is levied on its income. If there were no social dividend and no income tax the income which it would retain (measured up the vertical axis) would be equal to the income with which it started (measured along the horizontal axis). This relationship is shown by the straight line OA which is drawn at an angle of 45° so that the height up the vertical axis is at every point the same as the distance along the horizontal axis.

The straight line BC represents the relationship between income before adjustment (along the horizontal axis) and income after adjustment (up the vertical axis) if the family were paid a tax-freed social dividend equal to OB but were charged income tax at 50 per cent on all its other income. The line BC starts at the point B, which indicates that the family's income after adjustment would be equal simply to the social dividend OB if it had no other income. The level of this social dividend would, of course, depend upon the composition of the family, and would be greater the larger the family. The line BC slopes upwards with a gradient of 1 in 2, which represents the effect on post-adjustment income with a 50 per cent rate of tax, since, in addition to the fixed untaxed social dividend OB, the family can add to its retained income £1 for every £2 which it earns.

But the intelligent radical may well prefer a relationship of the kind shown by the broken line BDEF. The features of this line are that it starts at the same point B, or in other words the family is receiving the same tax-free social dividend as before. But on the first part of its earning it is taxed at a rate of 75 per cent instead of 50 per cent so that it retains only one quarter of its first earnings; and this is represented by the gradient of BD which is 1 up for every 4 units along. On the next slice of its earnings it is taxed at the rate of 40 per cent instead of 50 per cent, so that it retains 60 per cent of its additional earnings; and this is represented by the gradient of DE which is 6 up for every 10

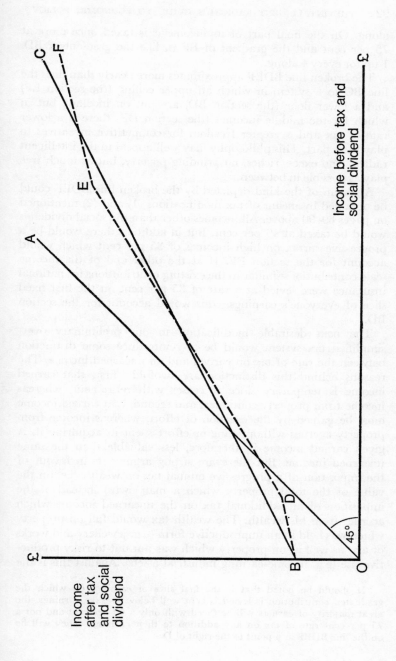

along. On the final part of its income it is taxed once more at 75 per cent and the gradient of EF is, like the gradient of BD, 1 up for every 4 along.

The broken line BDEF approximates more nearly than does the line BC to a system in which an upper ceiling (the section EF) and a lower floor (the section BD) are put on incomes, but in which for the middle incomes (the section DE) there is a lower rate of tax and a greater freedom for competitive incentives to play their part. This philosophy may well appeal to the intelligent radical : no excess riches, no grinding poverty, but as much free play as possible in between.

A system of the kind depicted by the broken line BDEF could be obtained by means of tax modifications (1) and (2) mentioned on pages 89–90 above. All incomes other than the social dividends would be taxed at 40 per cent. But in addition there would be a progressive surtax on high incomes of 35 per cent which would account for the section EF. If at the other end of the income scale contributions similar to the existing contributions for national insurance were levied at a rate of 35 per cent on the first fixed slice of everyone's earnings,[1] this would account for the section BD.

The next desirable modification to our preliminary over-simplified tax system would be to reintroduce some distinction between the rate of tax on earned and on unearned income. The reasons behind this distinction are twofold : first, that earned income is temporary since it ceases with retirement, whereas income from property continues; and second, that earned income must be gained by the exertion of effort, whereas income from property accrues without time or effort spent in acquiring it. A given earned income is, therefore, less valuable than the same unearned income. But there are strong arguments in favour of the imposition of a progressive annual tax on wealth (i.e. on the value of the total property which a man owns) instead of the imposition of an additional tax on the unearned income which accrues from his wealth. The wealth tax would fall on property which was held in an unproductive form (e.g. jewellery and works of art) as well as on property which was put out to risky productive use (e.g. income-earning industrial assets). Against this is the

---

[1] It should be noted that if the first slice of earnings on which the graduated contribution is levied is kept well below average earnings, the great majority of earners will be faced with only a 40 per cent and not a 75 per cent rate of tax on any addition to their earnings. They will lie on the line BDEF at a point to the right of D.

argument that a wealth tax is much more difficult to assess and to administer than is a tax on unearned income. But whether the tax be on unearned income or on wealth it will raise revenue and enable the standard rate of income tax to be that much lower.

Finally, there are a number of useful ways of extending the tax base so that the rate of tax which is needed to raise a given revenue can be reduced. It must suffice here to mention very briefly four possible cases.

First, there is the very important possibility (discussed on pages 71–72 above) of taxing the annual value of owner-occupied houses and of raising the rents of local authority houses to economic levels which would bring in additional revenue to the local authorities and make them less reliant on subsidies from the central government.[1]

Second, realised capital gains might (with some appropriate permission to average such gains over a period of years) be combined with other forms of income for assessment to surtax rates of income tax. Moreover, transfers of capital assets at death should be treated as realisations for capital gains purposes, whereas at present liability for capital gains tax is expunged whenever an asset passes at the death of the owner.

Third, there are a number of exemptions and remissions of various forms in the case of agricultural incomes and property for which there is little justification.

Finally, in the following Chapter we shall argue that there is a strong case for imposing taxes or other forms of charge or levy on activities which carry with them increasing threats of congestion, pollution, or the exhaustion of irreplaceable materials. Such activities positively cry out to be taxed on efficiency grounds, quite apart from the fact that any revenue raised from such taxation would make it less necessary to raise the standard rate of income tax in order to finance a social dividend scheme.

With graduated national insurance contributions on the first slice of earnings, with surtax rates on higher incomes, with a progressive wealth tax or, failing that, an additional tax on unearned incomes, and with a general broadening of the tax base, it should be possible to finance a full, comprehensive social dividend scheme without raising the standard rate of income tax above 40 per cent.

There is one further major set of modifications of the above tax proposals which the intelligent radical would welcome if they were

[1] The social dividend would, of course, be adjusted to take account of the market rent of dwellings.

practicable, namely to replace the progressive taxation of income by a progressive taxation of expenditure on consumption. As will be argued in the following Chapter, there is need to promote the community's saving for future generations; and the intelligent radical would wish to promote private savings and not simply to rely upon public savings through increased taxation and increased governmental surplus of current revenue over current expenditure. A tax on income discriminates against private savings, whereas a tax on consumption does not do so.

This can easily be seen by means of a simple numerical example. Consider a citizen with an income of £200 subject to an income tax of 50 per cent. His net disposal income will be reduced to £100. This he can spend on consumption or save. If he saves the £100 and if the rate of interest is 10 per cent, he will obtain a future income of £10 per annum, on which he pays income tax of £5. Thus by giving up £100 worth of consumption he obtains a future annual income of £5 a year – a net rate of return of 5 per cent in conditions in which the rate of interest is 10 per cent.

Consider the same citizen in the same conditions except that he is taxed at 50 per cent not on his income, but on his gross expenditure on consumption. If he spends his £200 on consumption, £100 of this will be taken in tax and he will, as before, obtain £100 worth of consumption goods valued at their cost price. If he saves the £200, he will not be taxed. Investing the £200 at 10 per cent, he obtains £20 per annum; and if he spends this £20 each year on consumption he will pay £10 a year in consumption tax and will obtain for his consumption £10 worth of consumption goods valued at their cost price. Thus by giving up £100 worth of consumption goods this year, he obtains £10 worth of consumption goods in future years, a rate of return of 10 per cent, which is equal to the market rate of interest.

It is the current level of consumption rather than the current level of income which measures the consumer's current standard of living and the amount of society's resources which he is thereby using up. Consider a wealthy man who is living on his capital which, as an extreme case, we suppose to be held in the form of jewellery on which no interest is earned. With an income tax he pays no tax since he has no income. With a progressive consumption tax he will pay tax on his consumption at a rate which rises progressively with the level of his consumption. The intelligent radical would welcome a consumption tax which will fall heavily on the wealthy man who consumes capital resources, but will fall lightly on the wealthy man who lives abstemiously and

saves resources which will be available for use by future generations.

Of course, wealth itself gives advantages of power, security,
and independence; and for this reason there is a strong case for
a tax on wealth itself. If such a tax exists – and the intelligent
radical would welcome it – the case for combining it with a tax
on consumption rather than with a tax on income is all the
stronger. For the wealth tax inevitably has the disadvantage of
penalising saving and encouraging the use of wealth to finance
current consumption; and this strengthens the case for a tax on
current consumption rather than on current income in order to
set up a counteracting encouragement to savings. A progressive
wealth tax combined with a progressive tax on consumption is the
best combination.

But is the change from a tax on income to a tax on consumption practicable? Let us consider this in terms of the three sections
of the curve BDEF in the Figure on page 91. This, as we have
seen, is composed of three elements : first, a single standard rate
of tax of, say, 40 per cent on all personal income other than the
social dividend; second, an additional surtax rate of, say, 35 per
cent on all such incomes above a certain level; and, third, an
additional levy of, say, 35 per cent on the first slice of all earnings,
a levy which would correspond to the existing graduated contributions to national insurance.

As far as the first element, namely the standard rate of tax,
is concerned, there are no insuperable difficulties in shifting from
a tax on income to a tax on consumption. The value added tax
(VAT) is in effect a tax on all goods and services purchased for
personal consumption. Provided, therefore, that the VAT is levied
at the same rate on all goods and services it can be used to replace
a standard rate of income tax by a corresponding standard rate
of consumption tax. Moreover the transition from the former to
the latter can be accomplished gradually simply by reducing the
standard rate of income tax and raising *pari passu* the rate at
which VAT is levied.[1]

[1] There is one arithmetical optical illusion which is worth noting.
Suppose from an income of £100 the tax man takes £40, leaving £60
to be spent on consumption. This represents a standard rate of income
tax at 40 per cent. The corresponding rate of VAT would, however,
be 66⅔ per cent. Thus on £60 worth of consumption goods (at cost
price exclusive of VAT) a rate of VAT of 66⅔ per cent must be levied
in order to add £40 in VAT to the £60 of cost-price goods to make up
£100 worth of consumption goods (at price inclusive of VAT). The rate
of income tax relates tax paid to *gross* income (inclusive of tax); the rate

As far as the second element mentioned on page 90, namely the surtax rate of income tax on high incomes, is concerned, the problems of shifting to a tax on consumption are more complicated, but not, one may hope, insuperable. A man's expenditure on consumption must be financed; and the money available for this consumption expenditure must be equal to his income plus his capital and similar receipts (e.g. realisation of capital assets by sale on the stock exchange) less the money which he spends on purposes other than consumption (e.g. purchase of securities on the stock exchange). To assess a citizen's expenditure on consumption for the purpose of a progressive tax on consumption would, therefore, involve assessing his income (which involves no additional problem, since this must be assessed in any case for an income tax) and, in addition, having an annual record of his receipts and outlays of money on capital and similar accounts. He would then be assessed to consumption surtax on his income plus the excess of his receipts over his outlays on capital and similar accounts. Such an assessment is clearly more complicated than an assessment which is confined to income. But for the purposes of the existing capital gains tax most capital and similar receipts and outlays must already be recorded. Moreover if there is to be a wealth tax there will need to be even more extensive recording of capital assets. Thus it should not be impossible to shift from a surtax on income to a surtax on consumption, particularly since the tax would be levied on only a limited number of rich persons.

But as far as the third element mentioned on page 90 (namely the graduated levy on the first slice of earnings) is concerned, the problems involved in shifting from a levy on earnings to a levy on consumption would seem to be insuperable. It would not be feasible to keep an accurate record of all the small capital and similar receipts and outlays for every member of the community, however poor, in order to translate earnings into consumption with the purpose of taxing the first slice of consumption at a specially high rate. At this end of the scale one would have to be content with a levy on earnings rather than with a levy on consumption.

The intelligent radical thus regards the following tax reforms as constituting an ideal rearrangement of fiscal principles :

(1) The abolition of corporation duty and its replacement by

of VAT relates tax paid to the *net* cost of consumption goods (exclusive of tax). The VAT rate of tax is thus always higher than the corresponding rate of income tax.

a progressive tax on the number of persons employed by any one employer (see pages 46–47 above).

(2) The payment of a weekly tax-exempt social dividend to everyone in the community on a scale corresponding to the existing supplementary benefit scale, this social dividend replacing all existing social benefits in cash and being automatically adjusted to a cost-of-living index in order to provide a given standard of real income.

(3) There would be a graduated levy corresponding to the graduated national insurance contributions expressed as a percentage of the first slice of earnings up to a given fixed limit.

(4) The standard rate of VAT, levied at the same rate on all goods and services for consumption without exception, would be gradually raised to replace the standard rate of income tax.

(5) A surtax would be levied on high levels of consumption.

(6) An annual wealth tax would be levied at a progressive rate on the size of large individual properties.

(7) An accessions tax would be levied on all sums received by way of gift or inheritance by an individual citizen, the rate of tax being the higher (a) the greater the total amount which the individual concerned had received up to date by way of gift or inheritance and (b) the larger the excess of the age of the giver over the age of the recipient.

There remains one further question of principle to be decided, namely the treatment of the family. In the case of a progressive tax should wealth, income, or consumption be taxed according to the amount of property, income, or consumption enjoyed by each individual member of the family separately or should the wealth, income, or consumption of each family be aggregated into a single family total for the purpose of determining the relevant rate of tax? The proposals made in this Chapter are based upon the principle that, wherever possible, each individual should be treated as an individual unit for tax purposes.

In the case of taxes on wealth this is a practicable principle. If the problem presented by property held in trust is so treated that the beneficial ownership of each piece of property is unambiguous, then a wealth tax can be assessed on the total amount of property owned by each individual and the rate of accessions tax can be calculated on the total amount of property which each individual citizen has received up to date in the form of gifts or inheritances. The result would, of course, be that tax burdens could be reduced by the wide spread of ownership among the members of a family. But this is as it should be. Two members of

G

a family each owning £50,000 should not be taxed at the same rate as a one-member family owning £100,000.

But as far as the taxation of income or, even more so, of consumption is concerned it would be appropriate to aggregate the total income or total consumption of a family, to divide this total by the number of members of the family,[1] and to determine the rate of progressive tax payable on the resulting averaged income or consumption per head for each member of the family. In doing this one would be recognising the impossibility of assessing separately how much of the total income or consumption in a family was in fact enjoyed by each individual member. The tacit assumption would be that each member consumed an equal share.[2] Subject to this conventional assumption, the principle would operate that each individual's wealth and income or consumption was separately assessed for the determination of progressive rates of tax.[3]

Would a reformed system of taxation of the kind proposed in this Chapter be administratively practicable?

In some ways the reforms would lead to administrative simplification. In the first place the weekly payment of a social dividend to every citizen instead of the present jumble of means-tested and other aids, while it would involve a large-scale weekly transfer of funds, would represent a much less complicated and much more straightforward operation. The separate administrations of personal allowances under the income tax, family allowances, graduated and ungraduated unemployment benefit, sickness benefit, old-age pensions, family income supplementation, supplementary benefits, rent rebates, rate rebates, and a host of other particularly means-tested schemes would largely disappear. Second, the elimination of the use of trusts as a means for obscuring the beneficial ownership of property would enormously

---

[1] Dependent children below a certain age probably have smaller needs than others and they might, therefore, properly count only as half persons for the calculation of income or consumption per head.

[2] Or, in the case of young dependent children, a half share.

[3] One important result of this principle would be greatly to reduce the tax burden on rich large families relatively to rich small families, since the possibility in a large family of dividing the wealth or income or consumption into a large number of separate packets rather than combining it into one large aggregrated packet for each family would, under a progressive tax system, greatly reduce the rates of tax payable by the members of the large family relatively to those payable by the members of the small family. We will return to this issue in the following Chapter (pages 121–122 below).

simplify the operation of all taxes which depend upon the assessment and control of capital assets, such as death duties, capital gains taxes, and a wealth tax.

But the proposals would introduce some new and difficult administrative problems. A shift from a progressive surtax on income to a progressive surtax on consumption would, as we have seen (page 96 above) in the case of rich persons involve the assessment not only of their annual income but also of the annual balance of their receipts and outgoings on capital account. An annual wealth tax would involve an annual assessment of the total value of each wealthy person's total property. An accessions duty would involve the recording for every individual (because any individual might in the end acquire much property by way of gift or inheritance) of all receipts (above some minimal exemption limit) of gifts or bequests accumulated over the course of his life.

It will be seen that all these major administrative problems centre round the recording and valuation of capital assets. At present these problems arise with estate duty when a man's property must be recorded and valued at his death and with capital gains tax when capital assets are bought and sold, in order to assess any rise in their capital values. But the problems would be on a much greater scale in the case of an annual wealth tax, since all the property, realised or not realised, of all wealthy persons, whether living or dying, would need continuous recording and valuing.

Two basic difficulties of such valuation would be much mitigated by the proposals made in this Chapter. In the first place, the elimination of the use of trusts to obscure the beneficial ownership of property would remove one of the great, perhaps the greatest, headache of all in the valuation of property for tax purposes. Second, the proposal made in Chapter V (pages 71–72 above) that all owner-occupied houses should for the purpose of taxation on income or consumption be assessed annually at their true rental value would provide a yardstick by means of which their capital value could be assessed for the purpose of a wealth tax and an accessions duty.

But many valuation problems would remain, in particular the valuation of private companies and the distribution of this total value among the different classes of private shareholder. These problems arise already in the case of the existing estate duty on properties passing at death, but their scale would be greatly increased by the need to value properties over a very much greater

range each year. Property valuation would become an even more important professional activity than it is at present.

There remains one final comment to be made on the fiscal reforms outlined in this Chapter. The introduction of the social dividend scheme and the changes in taxation proposed in this Chapter would incidentally provide effective instruments for carrying out the proposals made in Chapter IV for the regulation of trade union bargaining power (pages 59–61 above). We there proposed a scheme whereby a distinction could be drawn between those strikes and similar industrial actions which were, and those which were not, in support of excessive wage claims. If it were ruled that strikers and their families continued to receive the social dividend if their action were not ruled to be in support of an excessive wage claim, the bargaining power of trade unions in such cases would be greatly increased, since the very substantial proportion of their spendable incomes represented by the social dividend would continue unabated. On the other hand, the social dividend would be withheld from the workers and their families who were engaged in industrial action in support of an excessive wage claim,[1] and in this case the bargaining power of the trade union or similar organisation of workers would be dramatically reduced. Moreover, any strike pay made to the workers in such circumstances would be liable to the standard rate of tax levied on all income receipts other than the social dividend. Or, in so far as the transition from a standard rate of tax on income to a higher rate of VAT on consumption had been made, the expenditure on consumption of any strike pay or other funds would quite automatically be liable to consumption tax.

The proposals made in this Chapter, though they are devised solely for the redistribution of income, would thus incidentally be very helpful in any arrangements which were designed to increase the bargaining power of the trade unions in those cases in which their action was judged to be in support of wage claims within the established norm, but to reduce their bargaining power in support of claims in excess of that norm.

---

[1] There would be no intention to allow the families of such workers to be totally impoverished. There would have to be some special means-tested aid payable for the support of the wives and children concerned. But any such aid would be made in the form of a loan repayable later by the trade union or, failing that, the individual worker involved in the industrial action.

VII

Planning and Social Control:
Environment, Resources, and Population

We have now discussed the general principles on which governmental policies might be devised for three basic purposes : the
control of inflation (Chapter II), the promotion of a competitive
market mechanism to combine economic freedom with economic
efficiency (Chapters III and IV), and the redistribution of income
and property (Chapters V and VI). The emphasis throughout this
discussion has been upon the advantages of freedom of individualistic behaviour and decision in markets guided by the price
mechanism. But it has been a main purpose of those Chapters
to show that these advantages can be obtained only if the free-
enterprise system is operated against a background of appropriate
governmental interventions. In discussing these interventions the
emphasis has been put upon the construction of general fiscal
and monetary conditions in which the market mechanism could be
left free to work. To mention two examples, the stabilisation of
prices or incomes is to be achieved through the control of the
general level of taxation and of the total supply of money so as
to prevent inflationary or deflationary movements in the total
demand for goods and services, and personal incomes are to be
more equally distributed through the payment of a universal tax-
exempt social dividend to every citizen.

But man is a social animal as well as an independent individual ;
and the intelligent radical recognises that the Good Society
cannot be built without a number of particular social controls
in addition to the background of very general monetary and fiscal
conditions discussed in the preceding Chapters. Indeed in the
course of those Chapters passing reference has already been made
to at least three examples of very far-reaching particular interventions.

First, it has been noted (pages 51–54 above) that where economies of large-scale production are so marked as to leave room for
only one or a very few monopolistic productive enterprises (as in
the case of a railway network) it is desirable that the system should
be nationalised and made subject to close social control.

Second, it has been noted (page 15 above) that there are certain public goods (such as police for the preservation of law and order), the provision of which must be made for all citizens simultaneously, and that in such cases the particular goods or services in question must be provided through social, rather than individualistic, action.

Third, it had been argued (pages 72–73 above) that the provision of certain particular services (such as health services) cannot be left to the uncontrolled operation of market forces.

Such cases have been treated so far in this book in a very incidental manner. But the intelligent radical realises that the case for particular social interventions is much more pervasive than this cursory treatment suggests. In general, as we have seen, the market price mechanism beckons each citizen to do the best for himself by producing what other citizens want and will pay for; and it can for this reason be used as the underlying economic mechanism for the social co-ordination of the actions of individual citizens. But by no means all the repercussions of one citizen's actions upon another citizen's welfare can be properly ordered by means of a free enterprise price mechanism. The intelligent radical is acutely aware of the resulting need for a variety of particular social controls over particular aspects of economic activity. The need for such controls can be discussed under three closely related headings : Planning for an Uncertain Future; Structural Planning; and the Control of Social Costs and Benefits. In the rest of this chapter we will discuss each of these categories in turn.

(1) *Planning for an Uncertain Future*

Many economic decisions which must be taken today will be proved to be wise or unwise only by future events and in many cases only by events in the rather far distant future. Consider the construction now of a new steel mill. Whether or not it will prove to have been a wise investment will depend upon the price at which the steel which it will produce can be sold, the prices at which its inputs of fuel and raw materials can be purchased, and the wage at which its labour force can be engaged in each of the many future years in which the newly constructed plant will operate. In order, therefore, that the market price mechanism should work as an effective means for attracting present resources efficiently into the most profitable forms of investment in long-lasting fixed capital equipment, there would have to be markets which indicated what the prices of the relevant inputs and outputs were going to be at different future points of time.

The requirements of a fully efficient price mechanism are even more far-reaching that this, because they must take account of future uncertainties. Consider the cost in future years of the energy which the new steel mill will require for its operation. The future costs of various forms of energy may be greatly affected by future discoveries, whether these be 'geographic' discoveries (as in the case of the discovery of new oil fields) or whether these be 'technological' discoveries (as in the case of the control of nuclear fusion). The prospects for such basic discoveries are bound to remain uncertain; there is no conceivable price mechanism which will foretell the outcome.

Those persons who are responsible for the decision to build or not to build the steel mill must inevitably make up their own minds, on the best 'geographic' and 'technological' advice which they can obtain, what they think are the chances of the relevant discoveries. But having done so, they will want to know what effect these discoveries, if they were made, would have on the price of the energy supplies to the steel mill over the relevant span of future years. They could then make their decisions knowing what the relevant prices of their inputs and outputs would be ten years hence if the outcome of these discoveries had taken one course and what they would be if it had taken another course. Making their own estimates of the probabilities of the success of the various possible discoveries they could then make a reasoned decision about their present investment plans.

What would this involve in terms of a market price mechanism? Theoretically there could be a system of contingent forward markets in which people could today enter into contracts to buy and sell at predetermined prices a given commodity at a given future date contingently, i.e. on condition that certain discoveries or other specified events had occurred. Thus the steel producers could agree today to sell at a price fixed today a given quantity of a given quality of steel to be delivered in ten years time if, but only if, such-and-such discoveries or other specified events had occurred. By means of such a system of future contingent markets the plans for an uncertain future made by those who will have steel to sell in the future could be matched with the corresponding plans made by those who will need steel in the future. Buyers and sellers would know now what the prices would be to them in the future in different contingencies. They could make their plans reasonably and efficiently knowing that the demands and supplies in the future would be matched at these prices.

But such a development of contingent futures markets is in fact totally impracticable for two quite decisive reasons.

In the first place, the number of separate futures markets that would be necessary is clearly unmanageable. Every commodity for every future date and for every possible future contingency would require a separate market. There would be literally millions of relevant futures markets for each major decision-maker. The planners of the steel mill would have to buy and sell their many inputs and outputs each for a very large number of future dates each of which would be subject to a large number of separate contingencies. The system would be totally impracticable.

In the second place, even if all the relevant markets could be instituted, they would serve their purpose only if all buyers and sellers operated in them for all their purchases and sales. Otherwise the resulting future prices would not necessarily correspond to the prices which would in fact clear the market for all supplies and demands which would materialise when the future time was reached. But all future transactions cannot be covered now for the very simple reason that some of the people who may want to buy or to sell steel thirty years hence have not yet been born – or if born may still be at school. Since unborn babies and schoolchildren cannot be expected to operate now in future contingent markets for steel, the price system cannot be fully operated.

And yet there is a very important task of co-ordination to be performed even though it cannot be performed by the *laissez-faire* use of competitive free-enterprise price-mechanism markets. Those who are responsible for investing now in new steel mills will in fact be expecting to produce certain outputs of steel in the future. Those who are responsible for investing now in plants for the production of goods, such as motor-cars, which are made out of steel will be basing their plans on the availability of certain future supplies of steel. In the absence of a futures market how can the total plans of all the steel producers to supply steel in the future be co-ordinated with the total plans of all the steel users to use steel in the future?

There are many rough and ready ways of helping to co-ordinate plans for the future. The basic need is the exchange of information about plans so that, for example, the producers and users of steel can see whether the total supply that all the producers together are likely to produce in given circumstances is or is not much out of line with the total amount that all the users of steel are likely to want in those same circumstances. Something can be achieved simply by the publication and discussion in the press of plans for investment in individual industries. Forecasts can be made of what will be the probable future demand or supply of various products at different prices in different future conditions. Such forecasts can range in sophistication from a mere back-of-the-envelope calculation carrying past trends forward into the future to the scientific econometric forecasting models devised by professional research institutions.

But the government itself has an important role to play in these non-market methods of co-ordination of plans for the future.

In the first place, the government is one of the main users of future supplies of various products. It has plans for future expenditures on armaments, hospitals, schools, roads, and so on. Moreover, as the ultimate controller of the nationalised industries, it is responsible for future plans for the supply of many basic elements of transport and fuel. Co-ordination of future plans for the supply and demand of many important products would be hopelessly inadequate unless the government played a central part in the exchange of information about plans for future supplies and demands.

In the second place, non-market co-ordination of such plans requires centralised action. Some body is needed to receive and compare the various individual planned inputs and outputs. Moreover, these inputs and outputs are closely interwoven into a single pattern for the whole economy – coal, for example, being an input into practically every industry and, in turn, the production of coal depending upon inputs of equipment, transport, etc. from many other industries. Thus the co-ordination of future plans for inputs and outputs for all industries needs to be done as one single self-consistent exercise.

The government alone has the power to require those responsible throughout the economy for the many decisions about future plans to provide the relevant information; and it is itself one of the chief planners for the future of its own inputs and outputs. For these reasons there is a strong argument in favour of the government instituting a regular system of indicative planning by means of which the future course of the main markets for the main products in the main future contingencies can be traced.

There is one further and very important reason why this centralised task of co-ordination should be entrusted to the government. Exchange of information about plans by independent producers can very easily become a collusive monopolistic moulding of a single plan for the whole industry. Thus a meeting of independent producers of tools organised ostensibly merely to exchange information with consumers of tools about the way in which the total market for tools was likely to develop might end by a mutual agreement between the tool producers to reduce their planned outputs all round so as to obtain a high price for restricted future supplies. In the process of indicative planning there is a tight rope to be walked. On the one hand each independent competitive producer must know what his competitors as a whole are intending to do in order that the total indicative plan may be wisely formed. On the other hand, the competing producers must not jointly agree on a single restricted monopolistic plan. The surveillance of government is needed to see that information is exchanged without collusive joint monopolistic planning.

Such a system of indicative planning is only a process for the co-ordinated exchange of information which cannot be achieved by means of a market price mechanism. It does not require any independent decision-maker to adopt any particular plan; it merely helps him to choose a plan which is more likely to fit in with future market developments.

(2) *Structural Planning*

But we turn now to a case for central planning which goes much further than a mere exchange of information. We have just seen that the market price mechanism cannot be relied upon to cope with the problems of planning for an uncertain future. We turn now to a second major inadequacy of the price mechanism; it can cope very adequately with decisions whether a little more or a little less of this or that product should be produced, but it cannot cope adequately with structural decisions when it is necessary to decide whether a particular product should be produced on a large scale or not at all.

Consider two towns A and B between which there is no railway link. Should such a link be constructed? The price mechanism has a very useful function to perform in determining how much traffic there should be on the railway if it is built. If a charge is made for the rail journey between A and B equal to the extra cost imposed on the rail system by providing one more such journey, each individual traveller can decide for himself whether the value to him of making one more journey is worth the extra cost involved to the railway system in providing the extra journey.

If the railway is built, it will provide a large number of journeys; for since its construction involves a large capital outlay on the structural framework for the railway (track, tunnels, signals, stations, etc.), once it is built it will be available to provide for a considerable volume of traffic. In these circumstances the extra cost to the railway of providing one more journey will give no indication of the total cost of providing the large number of journeys which it is providing. Moreover the fare paid by the traveller for one more journey, while it will indicate how much he values taking one more journey, will give no indication of the value which he puts on the totality of all the journeys which he takes. The point can be illustrated by considering the price of an essential good, such as water. The cheap price charged for a gallon of water may indicate the value which a consumer puts on the last extra gallon of water which he uses to water his roses; but it certainly does not help to indicate how much value the consumer would place on the total amount of water which he consumes rather than go without any water – a value which is presumably very high indeed since without any water he would die of thirst. In a similar way the price which the traveller will pay for that last frivolous, but enjoyable holiday jaunt is no indication of the value which he places as a whole on the totality of his journeys which include the essential trips to market for his food and to the hospital for his health.

To decide whether the railway ought to be constructed involves a comparison of the total cost of providing all the journeys with the total value to all travellers of all their journeys. The total cost of the railway system may be estimated within a broad margin of error; the total value of the system to travellers is much more difficult to estimate. But in any case no market prices will indicate the correct answer.

The decision to build or not to build can, of course, be left to an uncontrolled free-enterprise decision on the part of potential private railway companies; but in that case there is no assurance that the correct decision will be taken. Only a public authority will have the motivation to attempt to estimate the total value to the travellers and the total cost to the system and to base its decision on the comparison of these two quantities.[1]

[1] Private enterprise will build the railway if and only if there is some volume of traffic on which it can expect to charge fares which enable it at least to cover the total cost of the system. But it is possible that the system ought to be built even if it cannot cover its total costs at any given uniform fare for travel, since the urgency of the limited number of essential journeys may mean that the total value to travellers is in fact very high. On the other hand, it is possible that the system should not be built even though it could cover its total cost; it may, for example, divert traffic from a competing road system which if it were underutilised

There are many instances of structural decisions of this kind for which the advantages of socially motivated public choice are so great that the intelligent radical would advocate bureaucratically planned decisions by public authorities rather than leaving decisions to unfettered private enterprise. The planning of road and rail networks is an outstanding example. Another example is the regulated use of land for various types of development under town and country planning schemes. We will discuss later some of the reasons for ensuring that different kinds of economic activity are concentrated geographically in different districts. Once this necessity is recognised it becomes a structural decision for some public authority to determine whether district A should be the industrial district and district B the residential district or vice versa.

But in principle this problem of structural adjustment is much more pervasive than is often realised. Two examples may suffice to make the point.

Suppose that it is possible to conceive of one hundred different models of small passenger motor-cars, but that because of the economies of large-scale production it is sensible to produce no more than five different models. Which five should be produced? Some consumers will prefer one model and some another; but all consumers have in fact to make their choice from the same limited set of five. The price mechanism will in fact provide no theoretically ideal answer to this question, since the loss of total value to the consumers who have to put up with model X (which is being produced) when they in fact would prefer model Y (which is not being produced) cannot be tested. There are no less than 75,287,520 ways of choosing 5 models out of a possible 100 models. There are, therefore, 75,287,520 structural forms of the car industry. Theoretically one might argue that some public authority should attempt to estimate the balance between total costs to the industry and the total value to all consumers for each of the 75,287,520 structural model choices open to the industry and then by regulation compel the industry to produce that particular combination of five models which gave the greatest excess of total value over total cost.

Or suppose that in some small village which is without a shop some enterprising person wishes to set up a village shop-cum-post-office. If it is at one end of the village street near the school it will be convenient for the village schoolchildren to purchase their

could carry the extra traffic at an additional cost lower than the total cost to the railway.

sweets; if it is at the other end of the village near the almshouses it will be convenient for the old-age pensioners to cash their old-age pensions. There is only room for one shop in the village. Theoretically the balance between total cost and total values of the two geographical structures for the village's shopping facility could be estimated and the shopkeeper required to go to the socially optimal end of the village.

Somewhere or another a line must be drawn between those cases in which a public authority should plan and regulate economic structures to achieve the best balance between total social values and costs and those cases in which the question is best left to the free entrepreneur in search of profit in spite of the fact that there is some element of structural choice involving total social values and costs. The intelligent radical puts much weight on free independent decision untrammelled by bureaucratic decision; he recognises that the pull of profit will often be in the socially desirable direction even when some element of structural choice is involved; he will remember that bureaucratic calculations are often wrong; and he will be very conscious of the temptation to corruption and bribery to which public servants are exposed when they have to settle by bureaucratic regulation matters which may make a considerable difference to the profits of those who are effected by their decisions. He will draw a line which will allow motor-car manufacturers to decide on their own range of models and village shopkeepers to choose their own position on the village street. But he will fully recognise and support the need for planned structural decisions by public authorities for such matters as transport networks or the town and country planning of the major geographical lay-out of human societies.

(3) The Control of Social Costs and Benefits

The price mechanism can carry out its task of beckoning resources into the production of things which consumers most want only if market costs properly measure the cost to society of producing the goods and if market prices properly measure the value to consumers of the goods which are produced. But in fact many social costs and benefits may elude the market mechanism so that a particular line of production may confer a benefit on some citizens for which those citizens are not charged or may impose a cost on society which the producers escape paying.

Some actions provide gratuitous benefits to third parties. A possible case is that of a farmer who by draining his own land indirectly improves the fertility of his neighbour's land as well as that of his own land.

But much more frequent and alarming are the cases where one man's action imposes costs and disadvantages on third parties without his having to pay for the damage which he does. A classic case is that of a factory which belches smoke and thereby causes dirt and damage to those who live in the neighbourhood; if no steps are taken, the producer concerned will not meet the extra laundry costs and the other inconveniences which his production imposes on those living in the neighbourhood of the factory. Another example is the use of nitrates as a fertiliser by farmers, the nitrates finding their way into the neighbourhood's water supply; unless special steps are taken, the farmers will not meet the cost of the damage done to the water supply. Unless special steps are taken, car owners who drive out on to the streets of a city during rush hour will not pay for the damage done by the fumes from their exhausts or for the cost of the extra delays caused to other travellers due to the extra congestion which they cause. Unless special steps are taken, producers will not bear the cost of the pollution which they may cause by discharging effluents into rivers or other waterways.

One could extend almost indefinitely this catalogue of possible forms of pollution of the environment through noise, stench, disposal of waste, congestion, and so on. Modern technological developments together with the crowding together of large populations has multiplied in a very marked manner the possibilities of particular lines of production imposing social costs upon the community for which the producer is not charged.

The intelligent radical stresses the need for measures to control the pollution of the environment. But in order that such control should be properly exercised it is necessary in the first place to assess the social cost involved by different forms of polluting activities. The assessment of these social costs raises a number of complex problems.

First and foremost there are the problems of deciding what are the probable ultimate polluting results of different forms of economic activity. For example, how deleterious to health is the presence of nitrates in the water supply? These are matters primarily for the natural scientist and the technologist.

Second, there is the problem of evaluating the social nuisance caused by a given degree of pollution of a given kind. How does one measure in money values the social cost of a given output of factory smoke when some people in the neighbourhood do not mind it much and others cannot stand it? Quite apart from the question how one adds up these different individual preferences, how does one discover them in the first place?

Third, a great deal of damage done through environmental pollution is future damage. The use of DDT may confer important immediate benefits without any immediate disastrous consequences; but it may be storing up great trouble for the next generation or the next generation but one. Quite apart from the technical difficulty in determining what will be the actual effects of this pollutant in the future, how does one evaluate that damage? How does one weigh the interests of future generations against the interests of the present generation?

It is not possible in this short book to analyse these problems of evaluation of social costs and benefits. In any case when all is said and done the assessment of the social damage in monetary terms must be of a rather rough-and-ready kind depending largely on the political judgement of the authorities concerned.

But some evaluation of the damage should be made because some such evaluation is inevitably implied in the control of pollution. For in the vast majority of cases it is not a question of prohibiting all pollution, but of keeping pollution down to an optimal level. Thus in the case of the smoking factory, it may be prohibitively costly to eliminate all smoke, but not too costly to reduce significantly the output of smoke. In this case to prohibit all smoke would leave the community without the smoke, but also without the product of the factory which may be very valuable to the consumers. To levy a charge on the factory equal to the evaluation of the social nuisance caused per unit of smoke might leave the community with some smoke nuisance, but also with some considerable output from the factory; and if the social nuisance caused by the smoke had been properly valued, this would be the preferable result.

There are different ways of exercising controls over pollution. In a number of cases the choice may lie between (1) a regulation prohibiting or limiting the amount of pollution (e.g. the amount of effluent discharged into a river), (2) a tax or other charge or levy on the amount of pollution (e.g. a levy per gallon of effluent discharged), and (3) the sale by auction of licenses or permits to pollute up to a given amount (e.g. the auctioning of licences permitting a total discharge of not more than x gallons of effluent per month).

The intelligent radical will wherever possible give preference to methods (2) or (3) over method (1) as a means of control. With method (2) the charge or levy per unit of pollution can be adjusted to the authority's valuation of the social damage done by the pollution; and thus the best balance between the social cost of the pollution and the desirability of continuing the economic process can be maintained. With method (3) the price which polluters will pay for the right to pollute can be compared with the authority's valuation of the social damage caused by the pollution, and thus the authority can decide whether the licenses which it is issuing have restricted the amount of pollution too much or too little, i.e. whether the price which the polluter is prepared to pay for the right to pollute is greater or less than the damage done by the pollution.

The use of methods (2) and (3) are thus applications of the methods of the market price mechanism to cover the case of social costs which would not otherwise have been brought into the market calculations. Thus, as we have seen in the previous paragraph, they have the advantage of pointing the way to the best balance between the advantages and the disadvantages of permitting a given level of some polluting activity. But they have also the other advantages of a use of the price mechanism. They allow individual producers freedom of independent action in deciding how much they will engage in the polluting activity, given that they will meet the social cost through the levy or licence fee which they must pay. Moreover, normally a tax or other charge on a noxious activity will be economically a much more efficient method of control than a direct regulation. Faced with a tax per unit of pollutant those who find it cheap to reduce pollution will reduce it more than those who find it expensive to do so; and thus a given reduction in the total pollution can be obtained at a lower cost than if each polluter was forced by regulation to restrict his pollution by the same amount. In addition, with a tax on pollution each polluter can employ the cheapest known method and, above all, will have every incentive to search for new and cheaper methods of pollution-abatement, whereas a direct regulation may well tie the polluter down to one particular method of abatement.

A further advantage of controlling pollution by means of a tax or other charge on the amount of pollution caused is that it will raise revenue. We have already made reference in Chapter VI (page 93) to this aspect of the matter. For this reason it is not only desirable to control pollution by taxing it rather than by regulating it in ways which raise no revenue, but it is also desirable to recognise the importance of taxing that which is most noxious rather than subsidising that which is less noxious. It is now generally recognised that motor transport in large cities is causing intolerable congestion, noise, danger to life and limb, and atmospheric pollution, and that private transport causes much more trouble per passenger-mile than does public transport. Both cause these troubles, but private transport causes more trouble than does public transport. The proper conclusion is to tax both forms of transport but to encourage public relatively to private transport by taxing private transport much more heavily than public transport. The wrong conclusion is to leave the taxation of private transport where it is, but to subsidise public transport in order to attract passengers from the private to the public sector.

In brief the sensible policy for the intelligent radical to advocate is that the authorities should make a grand tour round the whole economy taxing those activities which are socially costly according to the degree of social costs which they involve rather than starting to subsidies those activities which are somewhat less noxious socially. Such a policy would help to kill two birds with one stone : it would discourage anti-social activities and at the same time it would raise revenue required for the relief of poverty and for the large range of other desirable public expenditures.

For these reasons the intelligent radical will prefer to control pollution by levying a charge on the pollution rather than by a simple prohibition or quantitative regulation restricting the level of pollution, unaccompanied by any tax or charge. But the rule is not an absolute one. If the threatened social damage is sufficiently grave, it may be wiser and simpler to prohibit the offending activity entirely.

Moreover there will be cases where the best form of control is to regulate the structure of the economic activities concerned. One example of this is regulation of land use under rules for town and country planning to which reference has already been made (page 108 above). If smoking factories are confined to one district and residential dwellings to another, there will be no social cost of extra laundry bills. The smoke will not reach the housewife's clothes line. In such cases it is the interaction of two 'activities' (namely, factory production and residential dwelling) which gives rise to the social cost. When this is the case the best method of control may be to regulate the use of land in such a way that the two activities are kept apart from each other, so that there is no social cost to be met.

Serious environmental pollution is not the only phenomenon

H

which gives rise to serious concern for the future of society. The continued consumption of irreplaceable resources – coal, oil, minerals, etc. – the world's store of which is limited in amount must imply their ultimate complete exhaustion. This means in the end a final cessation of economic life unless substitute materials or methods of living can be found. The question which arises is whether this is simply a hard fact of life which must be stoically faced, reliance being put on the price mechanism to make the best of a bad job, or whether there are in this case also elusive social costs which mean that resources are not being conserved as well as they should be.

At first sight this problem would appear to be one in which an untrammelled use of the price mechanism would lead to the best use of the limited resources. As an irreplaceable resource becomes scarcer and scarcer, so the market price may be expected to become higher and higher. The expectation of higher prices in the future gives the owner of the resource an incentive to conserve it for sale later at the higher price. Moreover the rise in the price of the scarce resource causes every effort to be made to economise in the use of the resource. Thus when a mineral becomes scarce and its price goes up, it becomes profitable to work ores with a lower mineral content, to spend money on exploration of new sources, to use scrap and recycling processes more extensively, to substitute another raw material, to turn to the production of alternative final products which do not contain the mineral in question, and – above all – to direct research and development expenditures towards finding new ways of promoting all these various methods of reacting to the high cost of the scarce mineral.

Does this mean that there is no case for governmental intervention to conserve natural resources, since the market price mechanism can be relied upon to do all that can reasonably be done to conserve and to economise in the use of the scarce resource? There are in fact at least two types of reason why there may be a divergence between private and social costs in the use of a scarce natural resource and why, therefore, the public authorities should intervene in the interests of conservation.

The first case arises when the ownership of the resource itself is not clearly defined or is incapable of being effectively protected. Whaling presents a good example. Too intensive a catch of whales will cause the great beast to become extinct. If the whales in the oceans were owned, as it were, by individual farmers, they would not be so over-exploited. But as long as no one owns them as they swim about in the ocean and so long as there are a number of independent whalers, it will be to the interest of no individual whaler to conserve the stock of whales. If whaler A refrains, that simply means that whalers B, C, D, and E will have a better catch; it does not mean that whaler A will have a better future prospect of catching a whale. In such a case some public control on the exploitation of the resource is needed.

A similar example can occur if a pool of oil exists under an area of land owned in small parcels by a large number of owners and if the law gives the ownership of the oil under his land to the owner of each parcel of land. Landowners A, B, C, D, etc. are all then free to pump oil out of the single pool. If A refrains from pumping, that does not mean that A will have so much more oil to pump in the future. It means that B, C, D, etc. will be able to pump more oil. Thus no individual will have any incentive to conserve the oil. Each will pump oil as quickly as possible in order to obtain as large an amount from the common pool before the others can get at it. Once again some intervention by a public authority is needed for the conservation of the natural resource.

But even in the case in which this particular problem does not arise or has in one way or another been solved, there remains a general case for governmental action in the interests of conservation. This case rests upon a divergence between the private and the social future return to an act of present saving.

There are two ways in which a cut in present consumption can be used in order to enable consumption in the future to be increased.

The first method is the familiar one in which resources are used not to produce consumption goods now, but in order to produce machines or other capital equipment which will enable more consumption goods to be produced in the future. If the market rate of interest[1] is 10 per cent then private entrepreneurs will have an incentive to borrow £100 to purchase capital equipment this year only if the machine and its product will be worth at least £110 next year. The yield on the investment must be at least 10 per cent.

But if there is a heavy rate of tax on income from investment and/or on capital wealth, the private citizen who refrains from

[1] The argument is presented in terms of a stable level of money prices. The argument is in fact conducted in terms of the real rate of interest i.e. in terms of the money rate of interest minus the rate of general price inflation.

spending £100 on consumption goods this year will, with the rate of interest at 10 per cent, obtain less than £110 worth of consumption goods next year. The post-tax return on his savings will be less than the real rate of return to society on the capital investment which his savings would make possible. This gives rise to an obvious disincentive to abstain from present consumption in order to increase future consumption.

The second way in which abstinence from present consumption can be utilised in order to increase the possibilities of future consumption is by the conservation of exhaustible natural resources. If people refrain from consuming oil this year, there will be more oil available for consumption in future years. In this case too the divergence between the pre-tax rate of return to society and the post-tax yield to the saver works in a way analogous to the much more familiar case of investment in machinery and similar capital equipment which we have just examined.

Consider an exhaustible resource like oil which is becoming scarcer and scarcer and whose price is, therefore, expected to rise as time passes. Suppose that entrepreneurs expect its price next year to be at least 10 per cent higher than this year. Then by refraining from selling £100 worth of oil this year and conserving it they can sell it for at least £110 next year, thereby earning at least 10 per cent on the continued investment of the oil in the ground rather than its immediate sale for current consumption. If the market rate of interest is 10 per cent, entrepreneurs will find it worth while to borrow money to invest in oil-in-the-ground to hold till next year. But once again the existence of a tax on the interest received on their savings will mean that the savers who provide the money for the entrepreneurs to invest in the purchase of oil-in-the-ground obtain a post-tax return of less than 10 per cent on their savings. Once again the private post-tax return on savings is less than the real return to society of conserving oil, which has a social value of only £100 this year, for use next year, when it will be scarcer and have a social value of £110.

As we have already argued (see page 94 above), this divergence between the private and the social return on savings would disappear if taxation of income were replaced by the taxation of consumption.[1] Suppose that this were done and that with a market rate of interest of 10 per cent, the return to private savers in terms of postponed consumption were also raised to 10 per cent. A

---

[1] Assuming for the moment the absence of a wealth tax and of death duties.

consequential rise in private savings would mean that less was
spent on current consumption. This would cause a reduction in
the total level of money expenditures on goods and services; and
in order to prevent a general deflation of money demand it would
be necessary for the financial authorities to take steps to stimulate
the demand for capital goods. This could be done by a monetary
policy which reduced the rate of interest at which funds could be
borrowed.

This reduction in the market rate of interest would have a
double effect. In the first place, it would stimulate investment
in newly produced capital equipment, which is one way in which
the reduction in this years' consumption could be effectively used
to increase next year's consumption. But in the second place, it
would stimulate investment in oil-in-the-ground to carry oil over
from this year's to next year's consumption, or, in other words,
it would encourage the conservation in the ground of oil which
would otherwise have been pumped for use this year. This is a
second and equally effective way in which a reduction in this
year's current consumption standards can be used to raise next
year's standards. The additional conservation of this year's
oil for next year's use would make oil supplies scarcer this
year and more plentiful next year with the result that this year's
price would rise relatively to next year's price. The conservation
would be carried to the point at which the reduction in the
expected rate of rise of the oil price corresponded to the reduction
in the market rate of interest.

It is to promote developments of this kind that the shift from
the taxation of income to the taxation of consumption has been
advocated (see pages 94–96 above). But there is no prospect that
the divergence between the private return on savings and the social
return on investment can be entirely closed, since some elements
of this divergence will be maintained by the taxation of wealth
and of gifts and inheritances. And even if this divergence could
be entirely closed it would still remain an open question whether
the government should not give greater weight to the interests of
future generations than would be given by the individual private
saver, even if the saver received the whole social return on his
savings.

In the light of these considerations the intelligent radical will
recognise that there is a very strong case for supplementing private
savings with governmental public savings. This can be achieved
by means of a budgetary excess of tax revenue over current public
expenditures. The taxation will result in a reduction in private

consumption; the excess funds resulting from the budgetary surplus can be put on the capital market though the redemption of government debt; and the Central Bank can so order its monetary policy as to reduce interest rates to the extent necessary to ensure that these funds are effectively invested either in new machinery or in oil-in-the-ground.

Policies for the conservation of natural resources thus constitute one element in the general policy of restraining current consumption in order to make possible greater provision for future generations. But there is one reason for treating the conservation of exhaustible resources as a more basic element in this policy than the construction of new and additional machinery and other types of capital equipment. Deficiencies in the construction of machinery can be made good later. Deficiencies in oil-in-the-ground can never be corrected. It is much more important to be on the safe side in the case of oil-in-the-ground than in the case of the construction of new capital equipment. For this reason it may be wise to supplement measures for the promotion of savings and the reduction of interest rates with special measures to discourage the present use of exhaustible resources. An obvious measure is to impose specially heavy taxes on the use and consumption of such exhaustible resources.

So much uncertainty surrounds the possibilities of future environmental damage from the pollution caused by modern technologies and the possible difficulties of finding substitutes for scarce materials as they are exhausted that there is a strong case for a general shift of economic philosophy in order to play safe for the sake of our children and grandchildren.

The measures which have already been suggested above – taxes on polluting activities and on the use of exhaustible resources and measures to promote private and public savings – are of this kind. They will give a commercial incentive to free enterprise to select a structure of economic activities which avoids environmental pollution and the excessive use of exhaustible resources. But given the structural pattern of the economy, pollution and the exhaustion of natural resources will also be affected by the absolute level of total economic activity; and this means that there is a strong case for further restraint over both the rate of growth of population and, at least in the developed countries, over the rate of growth of consumption per head.

Much modern competitive business seeks new profitable openings for business by commercial advertising which aims at generating new wants or at making consumers desire to discard an old model of a product in order to acquire a new model of what is basically the same product. Thus the desire for higher levels of consumption of unnecessary gadgets and of new models to replace existing equipment is stimulated at the expense of taking out the blessings of increased productivity in the form of increased leisure. The discouragement of commercial advertisement by means of heavy tax on such advertisement and the return to broadcasting systems which are not basically the organs for the stimulation of new wants by advertisement (see Chapter V pages 49–50 above) would help to counteract these tendencies.

Moreover, some steps could be taken to give incentives to producers to produce more durable products rather than objects expressly designed to need rapid replacement. For example, if cars were taxed much more heavily in the first years than in the later years of their life, consumers would demand cars which were durable and did not need rapid replacement. The combination of taxation of exhaustible resources (such as metals) together with higher savings and consequentially lower rates of interest which we have advocated above would encourage the production of durable forms of equipment. In general, if a heavy tax is laid on the purchase of a piece of equipment and if this discouragement to purchase is offset by a reduction in the rate of interest at which the funds needed to finance the purchase can be borrowed, there will be an incentive to go for durability in the equipment. Less frequent replacement will mean a lower tax bill, and at the same time the value of the equipment's yield in the more distant future will be discounted at a relatively low rate.

The need to set some restraints on the levels of total production underlines the importance of the fiscal measures which we discussed in Chapter VI for the redistribution of income and wealth. If we wish to improve the lot of the poorest sections of humanity, then either we must rely on rapid and far-reaching growth of output per head or we must rely on the redistribution of income from the rich to the poor. In recent years both for the relief of domestic poverty and for the closing of the hideous gap between standards of living of the rich, developed countries and of the poor, underdeveloped countries the emphasis has been on economic growth. The extension of social services for the relief of poverty at home has, we have been told by our politicians, been impeded by the slow rate of growth of total output, it being assumed that any relief of poverty must come out of increased total production so that all classes may gain simultaneously. The raising of standards in the underdeveloped countries must, we have all assumed, come basically out of the growth of total world output, so that standards in the developed countries can be raised simultaneously with those in the underdeveloped countries.

The world cannot dispense altogether with further economic growth. Indeed a rise in output per head, hopefully of a less noxious form than in recent years, is an essential ingredient in the relief of world poverty. A glance at the arithmetic of national incomes is sufficient to show that it cannot possibly be achieved simply by a redistribution of income from rich to poor countries. But we would be wise to shift the emphasis significantly from a mere boosting of growth to a serious reliance on a more equal distribution of what we do produce, although we must face the fact that this inevitably multiplies possibilities of conflict of interest between different classes in society.

But as soon as we emphasise redistribution we are faced with a very difficult dilemma that if anything effective and manageable is to be done for the relief of poverty more help must be given to the large than to the small family (see page 89 above). However one may do this, whether by a social dividend of the kind advocated in Chapter VI or by more indirect and disguised means, it necessarily involves subsidising the production of children. If we aim at shifting our philosophy from a mad scramble for ever higher levels of production and consumption of goods, however unnecessary they may be, to a more humane and compassionate society in which basic needs are assured, if necessary at the expense of inessential luxuries, we come up against the thought that our children, who by the way never asked to be born, are also human beings with basic needs and that the more there are of them in a family the greater the total needs of that family if every member is to be given a proper start in life.

The same basic dilemma shows itself in a somewhat different form when we consider the closing of the gap between the rich and the poor countries. It is the poor countries with the highest rate of population growth which will be in the greatest need of foreign aid and technical assistance in order to undertake those projects of capital development (building new schools, new hospitals, new houses, new machines, new tools and so on), which are necessary simply in order to prevent a decline in the amount of capital equipment per head of the population. However disguised, this amounts in fact to the international subsidisation of those countries which are producing the most children.

Restraint on consumption per head is a means of restraining total demands on scarce resources which necessarily involves restraints on standards of living. On the contrary, restraint of population growth is a means of restraining total demands without any fall in standards of living.

But while the control of population might make the most desirable contribution to the control of the total demand on resources, it presents in one way the most difficulty in its achievement. The price mechanism together with a proper, extensive system of pollution taxes by imposing appropriate pecuniary penalties can be used to restrain scarcities of material and environmental goods; these instruments provide powerful negative feedbacks in the total dynamic system. As the demands on material and environmental resources become excessive, so prices and charges rise to discourage demand and encourage supply. But with population, alas, it seems that we must introduce a vicious positive feedback. We wish to discourage large families; but on distributional grounds the larger the family the more we must subsidise it. This means that for distributional reasons we are introducing a divergence between the private cost to the parents and the social cost to the community of feeding, housing, clothing, educating, and caring for the health of children. Can anything be done to offset this?

One possible way out of this dilemma is to devise population policies which restrain population growth by means other than pecuniary penalties on the production of children. The first thing obviously is to enable everyone to avoid having more children than they want. Sterilisation and abortion on demand, the development of family planning advice and services in all maternity hospitals, the complete incorporation of universal and free family planning into the National Health Service, the provision of extensive domiciliary family planning services, school education which inculcates that sexual intercourse should never take place without contraception unless a child is positively planned, governmental promotion of research into contraceptive methods – these are the first types of action to which we must devote resources to match any help which we give to large families.

Thus we must subsidise large families on distributional grounds, but must restrain any resulting population growth; and so we advocate measures to make contraception readily available to every citizen and to ensure that everyone recognises the irresponsibility of producing an unwanted child. But in Chapter V (pages 80–81) we showed the desirability on distributional grounds of the fortunate having somewhat larger families than the unfortunate and pointed out that success in breaking down social barriers would make such an element of differential fertility even more advantageous. Accordingly in Chapter VI (page 98) we suggested a form of taxation of the rich which fell with especial weight on childless and small families. This combination of measures may serve well to cope with the demographic problems of a country like the United Kingdom where fertility rates have already fallen and are no longer much higher than is necessary to replace the population. The intelligent radical will wait and see how effective they are before contemplating the possible need for further measures designed to influence population trends.

In this Chapter we have considered three groups of reasons why the market price mechanism cannot be expected to lead to the most efficient use of society's resources : it cannot cope fully with the uncertainties of the future; it cannot give the correct guidance for structural changes in the economy; and it overlooks many social costs and benefits which escape its calculus. To a smaller or greater degree these inadequacies pervade practically all economic activities. A housewife purchases a durable washing machine in the absence of a forward market for outside laundry services to inform her that in fact the charges for outside laundry services are going to fall so much that she would do better to send her dirty linen out to be washed. A villager decides to set up shop at one end of the high street without any authority doing the intensive cost-benefit analysis to determine that as a matter of fact the other end of the high street would have been socially more beneficial. A man puts on a highly coloured tie without making payment to his sensitive neighbour whose aesthetic sense is thereby offended.

Perhaps Plato was correct after all. We need benevolent guardians to tell us what goods to purchase, where exactly to live and have our business, and how to dress. It is not difficult to make out a respectable intellectual case for the most extensive form of authoritarian socialist society to regulate all the actions of that social animal, man.

The intelligent radical recognises this case, but repeats the age-old question : Who will guard the guardians? If one wanders too far down the socialist path freedom disappears, the costs of bureaucratic controls mount, and among the innumerable guardians will be found many fools and many knaves. The end result of the authoritarian society is as horrible as the end result of uncontrolled *laissez-faire*. The intelligent radical seeks for some intermediate position in which the maximum possible use is made of the market price mechanism, as the foundation on which a structure of essential social controls is built.

Sir Winston Churchill once said of democracy that it was the worst possible form of government except the others; and Mr E. M. Forster in the same vein wrote a book entitled *Two Cheers for Democracy*. The intelligent radical is anything but an optimistic utopian. He recognises that the world is a wicked place in which compromise is inevitable. He freely admits that the price mechanism is the worst possible form of economic system except the others, and his stirring political rallying cry is : Two Hearty Cheers for the Price Mechanism.

VIII

The International Setting:
(1) *The Price Mechanism at Work*

The preceding Chapters have all been written without reference
to the balance of payments, commercial policy, or any other
financial or economic relations with the rest of the world. It is
the main purpose of this book to discuss the domestic economic
problems and policies of a country like the United Kingdom, that
is to say, to consider how such a country can best put its own
house in order. But it would be ridiculous to reach any con-
clusions about what was the best set of domestic policies for a
country like the United Kingdom without considering them in
their international setting. This we intend to do in this and the
following Chapter.

Up to this point our advice to the intelligent radical has been
to regard an efficient market price mechanism as the basic economic structure for the sort of society which he would favour,
and then to consider what interventions are necessary to preserve
full employment, to prevent inflation, to achieve an equitable
distribution of income and property, to deal with inevitable
monopolies and public goods, to plan for an uncertain future,
and to cope with divergences between private and social costs and
benefits.

We will discuss the international setting in a similar manner.
We will first outline in the present Chapter what are the necessary
basic steps to ensure the efficient operation of a market price
mechanism internationally; and we will then in the following
Chapter consider what governmental interventions are desirable
for the control of this international market mechanism. But in
the discussion of both of these matters – both the construction of
the basic international market mechanism and also the range of
desirable controls over the operation of that mechanism – we shall
have to draw a distinction between what the government of a
country like the United Kingdom can do alone and what can be
achieved only by international agreement between a number of
such governments.

A country like the United Kingdom which was adopting a set

of domestic policies of the kind discussed in the preceding Chapters of this book could unilaterally go far towards integrating its own domestic market with world markets by taking two decisive steps. It could adopt a policy of free trade for its commerce with the rest of the world and it could allow the exchange rates between its own currency and the currencies of other countries to float in a free market for foreign exchange.

We have already in Chapter III (page 49) considered some of the advantages of a policy for the free and unimpeded import of goods and services from abroad. It would be one of the most effective means for ensuring competitive market conditions domestically. A productive concern, because of the economies of scale, may have to produce an output which is large relatively to the domestic demand for its product; but any resulting mono-polistic power which it might thereby exercise would be greatly curbed if it had to compete freely with foreign competitors. It may be old fashioned to argue that free trade promotes efficiency and so welfare by inducing domestic producers to produce the things in which their costs are relatively low and by leaving consumers free to buy from abroad the products in which the costs of the foreign producers are relatively low, but that does not make the argument incorrect or unimportant.

The protection of a particular line of production against foreign competition is sometimes defended as a method of ensuring a decent standard of living for the domestic producers concerned. But the intelligent radical will recognise that this is only a parti-cular form of the argument for controling prices in order to affect the distribution of income, an argument which has already been discussed and dismissed in its domestic setting (see pages 68–72 above). There is no more case for levying a charge on the import of wheat in order to keep up the rental value of arable land or the wages of the farm labourer at the expense of the consumer of bread than there is for controlling the rent of houses to improve the lot of the tenant at the expense of the landlord. In both cases it is preferable simply to help the poor at the expense of the rich by means of the general measures discussed in Chapters V and VI.

But if the country allows complete freedom of imports, by what mechanism can it ensure that it is exporting enough to pay for all the imports which its consumers will choose to purchase? How, in other words, is it to look after its balance of payments? It is here that variations in the price of foreign currencies in terms of the domestic currency will play their part in integrating the domestic and the world markets for goods and services. Suppose that the United Kingdom, having adopted the intelligent radical's advice on its domestic policies, finds that it has a deficit on its balance of payments. Those with pounds sterling who wish to acquire foreign currencies to finance the purchase of imports and to make other payments abroad will outweigh the foreigners who with their foreign currencies wish to purchase pounds sterling to finance their purchases of United Kingdom exports and to make other payments to United Kingdom residents. The pound sterling will depreciate. The price of imports will go up relatively to the price of home produce in the United Kingdom, because more pounds must be paid to obtain a given amount of foreign currencies and of foreign goods while domestic prices and incomes reckoned in pounds sterling have been stabilised by the measures discussed in Chapter II. In foreign markets the price of United Kingdom products will fall relatively to the price of the foreigners' own domestic products, since the foreigner will have to give a smaller amount of his currency to purchase a given number of pounds' worth of United Kingdom goods.

The consequential shift in the United Kingdom from expensive imports to cheap domestic produce will cause a shift of demand from foreign imports to home-produced substitutes in the United Kingdom. The consequential shift in overseas countries from their own relatively expensive produce to relatively cheap United Kingdom products will cause a shift of demand on to United Kingdom exports. The United Kingdom economy will be affected in two significant ways.

In the first place, the volume of its imports will fall and the volume of its exports will rise. If this movement is on a sufficient scale – and we will return to this question later – the deficit on the United Kingdom's balance of payments will be removed.

Second, there will be a net inflation of the amount of money expenditure on United Kingdom products partly because residents in the United Kingdom are shifting their demand from expensive imports to relatively cheap home-produced goods and services and partly because foreigners are increasing their demands for United Kingdom exports. In order to prevent this expansion in the demand for United Kingdom products from causing an inflation of domestic prices and incomes in the United Kingdom, the financial authorities, on the principles discussed in Chapter II, will have to take fiscal and/or monetary measures to restrict other expenditures in the United Kingdom.

The combined result of these developments would be : (1) a restriction by the financial authorities of total domestic demand which would release resources in the United Kingdom to produce additional goods for additional export or for the replacement of imports from abroad; and (2) a depreciation of the exchange rate which, by making United Kingdom products cheaper relatively to foreign products, would cause the foreigner to purchase additional exports and the home consumer to replace imports of foreign goods with home-produced goods.

We may summarise the basic principles upon which this integration of the domestic market mechanism with foreign markets is achieved in the following way. There are three objectives or 'targets' of overall economic policy : Stability of Money Prices and Incomes, Full Employment, and a Balance of International Payments. There are also three market instruments or 'weapons' of overall economic policy : Financial Policy, Wages Policy, and Exchange Rate Policy. The system which we are advising the intelligent radical to advocate is : (1) that the overall level of demand for home produced goods should be so controlled through Financial Policy (i.e. through fiscal policy and monetary policy) as to maintain Stability of Money Prices and Incomes; (2) that Wages should respond to the demand for labour so as to ensure Full Employment, given the stabilised level of money demand for the products of labour; and (3) that the Rate of Exchange should respond to the demand for foreign currencies so as to ensure a Balance of International Payments for imports and exports and similar transactions, given full employment and a stable level of domestic prices and incomes internally.[1]

[1] One can, of course, outline the system in terms of more than three major objectives; but in order to obtain an efficient and workable system one must add at least one independent 'weapon' of policy for each additional 'target' of policy. For example, if one wishes to add as a 'target' the maintenance of a desirable balance between society's current consumption and its savings for the future, one must break Financial Policy down into the two 'weapons' of Fiscal Policy and Monetary Policy. Given any stabilising level of total expenditure one can then raise taxes (under Fiscal Policy) and lower interest rates (under Monetary Policy) if it is desired to reduce current consumption and to stimulate the investment of a corresponding amount of savings. One then has four 'targets' (Stability of Money Prices and Incomes, Proportion of National Income Saved, Full Employment, and the Balance of Payments) matched by four 'weapons' (Fiscal Policy, Monetary Policy, Wage Policy, and Exchange Rate Policy). One could then add another 'target' such as an

It is worth noting that in these conditions a general price inflation cannot be imported from abroad. Suppose a general inflation
of prices to continue in all countries except the United Kingdom
which, by the methods discussed in Chapter II, successfully
stabilises an index of domestic money prices or incomes. If the
exchange rate between the pound sterling and foreign currencies
were fixed, the system could not be maintained. The price of
imports would rise in line with the inflation of prices in the rest
of the world. If United Kingdom prices did not rise, there would
be an endless shift from foreign products on to United
Kingdom products both by foreigners and in the United Kingdom itself. But if any such excess demand for United Kingdom
products was allowed freely to lead to a rise in the price paid
for pounds in terms of foreign currencies, import prices would
not rise in the United Kingdom, the rise in the price of imports
in terms of foreign currencies being offset by the rise in
the amount of foreign currencies which could be bought with a
pound.[1]

The story is, of course, different if the trouble is not a general
overall inflation of money prices in the rest of the world, but a
rise in the price of the things which the United Kingdom imports
(oil, foodstuffs, metals, etc.) relatively to the things which she
produces at home and exports (manufactured products). If this
rise in the price of imported products relatively to home produced
products is due to external world developments, the United Kingdom cannot avoid its consequences. The price of imports and so
the cost of living will rise even though the price of domestic
produce is stabilised (see pages 32–33 above). The consequent reduction in the standard of living cannot be avoided; society as a

Equitable Distribution of Income, in which case Fiscal Policy must be
divided into two 'weapons' such as the level of the Social Dividend and
the level of the Standard Rate of Income Tax suggested in Chapter
VI. There is in fact no end to this enumeration of more and more
detailed objectives; but in order to ensure that the proposed system is
a workable one it is useful to think in terms of the addition of a further
independent 'weapon' of policy to cope with each additional policy
'target'.

[1] One of the tragedies of recent years has been the fate of Germany
which was for so long successful in combining a financial policy for
domestic price stabilisation with a wage policy for full employment. But
by refusing to allow the mark to float freely and to appreciate without
limit as the other countries of the world inflated, Germany was in the end
compelled to import these external inflationary forces. If only Germany
had been willing to combine her domestic policies with a freely floating
mark, what an example might she not have set!

whole is obtaining less imports for each unit of its products which it exports.[1]

The price mechanism outlined above for maintaining equilibrium in the balance of payments will, however, work only if the demand for United Kingdom products is sufficiently sensitive to price changes. Suppose that the balance of payments is in deficit and that as a result the pound depreciates. This will raise the price of United Kingdom imports in terms of the pound sterling; consumers in the United Kingdom will purchase less imports; less foreign currency will be needed, therefore, to finance the country's imports; but if the United Kingdom's imports are not very sensitive to the price change, the saving in the amount of foreign currency needed to finance the import bill may be small. As far as the country's exports are concerned, the depreciation of the pound will lower the price of United Kingdom exports in terms of foreign currencies; the foreigner will purchase more goods from the United Kingdom, and if the foreigners' demand is sensitive to the price change, the amount of foreign currency spent on United Kingdom exports will be increased; but if the foreigners' demand for United Kingdom produce were very insensitive to price changes, the increase in the quantity of United Kingdom exports might be less than sufficient to make up for the fall in their price in terms of foreign currency, in which case the foreign customers would be spending a smaller amount of foreign currency on United Kingdom exports. Thus if the United Kingdom's demand for imports and the foreigners' demands for United Kingdom exports were both very insensitive to price changes, the result of the depreciation of sterling could be that there was a very small reduction in the United Kingdom's import bill in terms of foreign currency and that the United Kingdom's receipts of foreign currency from the sale of exports fell by as much as this small fall in the import bill. The exchange rate variation would not have been effective in restoring equilibrium to the balance of payments.

Given time for the changes in relative prices to work out their effects upon consumers' demands, there is no reason to fear in-

---

[1] The distribution of the consequential burden can, of course, be affected by fiscal policy. Thus if, in order to prevent a decline in the standard of living of the poorest members of society, the money social dividend proposed in Chapter VI were linked to the cost of living it would have to be raised as the price of imports rose. In this case the standard rate of income tax (or some other tax) would have to be raised in order to finance the higher money cost of the social dividend.

I

adequate price sensitivity in the case of countries like the United Kingdom. Countries of this kind all produce a large range of industrial products which compete with one another – United Kingdom cars with German, French, and Italian cars for example. Changes in relative prices do therefore ultimately cause appreciable substitutions between the products of different countries of this kind. The ultimate effect of changes in relative prices will be to restore equilibrium to balances of payments.

But these shifts of demand from one country's products to another's may take some time. Consumers will shift from the high to the low-priced source of supply only gradually as the price changes work their way into the shops, as consumers realise the implications of these price changes, and as they can make suitable rearrangements in their use of different products. The immediate effect of a depreciation of the pound may well be to worsen any deficit on the United Kingdom's balance of trade. If imports are not immediately reduced, the import bill in terms of foreign currency will not fall. If exports are not immediately increased, the receipt of foreign exchange from the sale of exports will fall because of the reduction in their price in terms of foreign currencies. The balance of trade will thus deteriorate. But as time passes United Kingdom consumers will replace imports with domestic produce, and foreigners will increase their purchases of United Kingdom exports. In due course the change in prices will have the appropriate effect in improving the balance of trade.

During this period of adjustment the action of speculators in the foreign exchange markets is of crucial importance. Consider the following developments. The balance of payments is in deficit; the pound depreciates; at first this worsens the deficit and the pound depreciates still further; a point is reached at which the prices of United Kingdom products have become so excessively low relatively to the prices of foreign products that a considerable surplus on the balance of payments will result as soon as these very great changes in relative prices have had time to lead to the consequential great shifts in the volume of the country's imports and exports. The question at issue concerns the nature of the reactions of speculators in foreign exchange to a situation of this kind. Will they sell pounds to buy foreign currencies or will they sell foreign currencies in order to support the pound?

If they sell pounds they will intensify the depreciation of the pound and make matters worse. But if they buy pounds with foreign currencies they will be performing a useful and essential social function. Their speculative purchases of pounds with foreign currencies will enable United Kingdom importers to sell their pounds to obtain foreign currencies for the finance of imports during the period of time while the relative price changes are having their delayed effect in expanding United Kingdom exports and contracting her imports.

If the authorities are successful in carrying out the domestic measures suggested in Chapter II for the stabilisation of the general level of domestic money prices and incomes, the action of foreign-exchange speculators will undoubtedly be of this socially useful character. Suppose that the gnomes of Zürich or other persons who own foreign currencies are certain that the pound price of United Kingdom products will not be inflated. When the pound has depreciated to a degree which makes United Kingdom goods excessively cheap relatively to foreign goods, foreign speculators will be certain that in due course the United Kingdom's balance of payments will move into a surplus condition, the commercial demand for pounds will exceed the supply, and the pound will appreciate. By buying depreciated pounds now, the foreign speculator will be able to make a profit by selling them at an appreciated value in the future. He will be paid for the socially useful task of providing foreign currencies to the United Kingdom during the transitional period in which the balance of payments is in the process of adjustment.

But suppose that the policies for the stabilisation of domestic money prices and incomes had not been adopted. When the pound depreciated as a result of the initial deficit on the balance of payment, the price of imports and the cost of living would rise. Suppose that any rise in the cost of living led to a corresponding rise in money wage rates and that, in order to implement a domestic policy for full employment, this rise in money wage costs was accompanied by a financial policy which led to a corresponding rise in money expenditures and in the prices of domestic products. All domestic money prices, costs, and incomes would start on an inflationary spiral. This rise in domestic prices and costs would cause people to expect ultimately a still greater shift from United Kingdom goods on to foreign goods; and this expectation of an ultimate worsening in the balance of payments would give rise to the expectation of an ultimate increase in the strain on the balance of payments with the consequential further depreciation of sterling. Any domestic or foreign speculative owners of pounds sterling would sell them in the expectation of a further depreciation in their value in terms of foreign currencies.

These speculative transactions would increase instead of relieving the initial pressure on the balance of payments.

These speculative considerations provide one of the most compelling reasons why the intelligent radical advocates a financial policy designed to stabilise the general level of domestic money prices and incomes. In addition to the advantages for domestic accounting purposes from having a currency with a stable real purchasing power (advantages which have been examined at length in Chapter II), the possession of such a currency immensely lessens the country's balance-of-payments problems. If there is complete assurance that domestic inflations will be avoided, there will be very powerful market speculative forces stabilising the exchange rate around its equilibrium value. If the rate is appreciably depreciated beyond its long-run value, speculators will support the currency; and they will sell it, if it appreciates markedly above its long-run value.

As we have seen, the ease and speed with which the mechanism of exchange rate variations will restore equilibrium to the balance of payments depends upon the degree of sensitivity of foreign, as well as of domestic, consumers to changes in the relative prices of United Kingdom and of foreign products. There are many ways in which this sensitivity can be encouraged but which depend upon international agreements for their implementation.

Clearly the United Kingdom's exports will be able to expand in foreign markets as a result of a relative fall in their price only if the foreign governments adopt a commercial policy which permits such an invasion of their domestic markets. It is for this reason of great importance to countries like the United Kingdom to seek a general commercial agreement among all such countries to allow the free import of goods and services from each other.

For this reason the intelligent radical advocates support for an international agreement among all developed industrial countries by which they all admit the free import of goods and services from all sources. In so far as their mutual trade is concerned, such an agreed free-trade policy would remove all artificial barriers against readjustments of imports and exports in response to changes in relative prices. At the same time the developed, industrialised countries would admit freely all the products of the less developed, unindustrialised countries without insisting that their own products should in return be freely admitted into the markets of the less developed countries. These latter countries could still protect their infant industries, a policy requirement which is unnecessary in the case of those countries which are already industrialised.

This freeing of the channels of trade by the developed countries should not be confined simply to the removal of import duties and import quotas. The international agreement for any such extensive freeing of trade should cover other less obvious methods of giving protection to domestic producers against foreign producers. It is not possible in this book to consider in detail the matters which would need to be covered in any complete code of trade conduct by the members of a universal free-trade club of developed countries, though we shall have occasion later to refer to one or two particular issues (see pages 140–141 below). Two outstanding points should, however, not go unnoticed.

In the first place, public expenditures on goods and services financed out of governmental budgets now constitute a very substantial proportion of the total demand for goods and services in each of the main industrialised countries. It is, therefore, of the first importance that governments themselves should agree to buy in the cheapest market and not to refrain on protectionist grounds from shifting from the purchase of domestic to the purchase of foreign products if the latter are cheaper than the former.

Second, the governments of the developed countries themselves make foreign loans and give direct aid to other countries. The sensitivity of trade to changes in relative prices can be appreciably increased if all such loans and grants of aid are made in the form of money payments which can be spent in any market. Thus suppose that the United Kingdom is in deficit and Germany is surplus on its balance of payments; and suppose that the German government was giving aid to the government of Israel. The correction of the balance of payments between the United Kingdom and Germany could be eased if, as the pound depreciated and the mark appreciated, the Israeli government could sell the marks received from Germany to the United Kingdom importers of German products in order to acquire pounds to purchase goods from United Kingdom exporters instead of from German exporters. It should be part of any general agreement that loans and aid should be made in freely convertible currencies and should not be tied to the purchase of the products of the lending or grant-giving country.

Such a grand international agreement of this kind for the simultaneous adoption of free-trade policies by all the developed countries would make the channels of international trade much more sensitive to changes in relative prices.[1]

[1] The intelligent radical will recognise that it is one of the tragedies of the last decade that just as opinion in the United States was moving

But this greater sensitivity to relative prices will help with the adjustment of international balances of payments only if relative prices move in the correct way, that is to say, only if the prices of the products of the deficit countries are allowed to fall relatively to the prices of the products of the surplus countries.

Such desirable price adjustments would occur as a natural result of market forces if (1) the authorities in each country adopted successful financial and wage policies which stabilised their own domestic economies, (2) exchange rates were allowed to float freely without any governmental intervention, and (3) as a result private speculators supported any currencies which were temporarily depreciated more than was needed for long-run equilibrium.

An international monetary problem would arise only if these conditions were not fulfilled. In particular a problem may arise because national governments may intervene in foreign exchange markets. A national government acting through an exchange equalisation account may, in the manner of private foreign-exchange speculators, itself support its national currency by selling its holdings of foreign currencies in the market in order to buy up its own national currency or it may accentuate any depreciation of its own currency by selling its own currency in the foreign exchange market in order to purchase foreign currencies to add to its holdings of foreign reserves in its exchange equalisation fund.

National authorities may indulge in such interventions for a variety of reasons. Some of these interventions may be very desirable. If, for example, private speculators for good or bad reasons do not believe that a national government will control a runaway domestic inflation, then (as explained on page 131 above) instead of supporting the currency concerned when it starts

perceptibly in support for a grand Free Trade Area of all developed countries, the United Kingdom became entangled in negotiations to join the European Economic Community part of whose basic philosophy was to form a regional Customs Union with protective tariffs against imports from all outsiders. The intelligent radical will urge the United Kingdom government to put first things first and to insist that the European Economic Community drop this unnecessary protective attitude. Free import from all sources into the European Economic Community would also incidentally release the United Kingdom from the shameful obligation which it has undertaken to give preferences to European products over Commonwealth products – to take butter on better terms from the French peasant than from the New Zealand farmer, beet sugar on better terms from the German peasant than the cane sugar from Mauritius and the West Indies, textiles on better terms from Italy than from India.

to depreciate they may well sell it and thus themselves feed the inflationary pressure which is the cause of their fears. A national government may intervene in the foreign exchange market in order to offset such perverse speculative movements. Or, to take a less extreme example, private speculators may not go to this extreme of selling a currency which is under temporary pressure; they may simply fail to support it. In this case a national authority may properly wish to fill the blank and play the role of the absent useful private speculation by supporting the national currency during its temporary period of excessive weakness, while changed price relationships are allowed gradually to exercise their beneficial role on the balance of payments.

But national governments can also misuse their powers of intervention in foreign exchange markets. Suppose that a government wishes to give fuller employment to its labour force, but that instead of adopting appropriate domestic measures (such as those discussed earlier in this book) it attempted to expand its export markets in a way which was not required on balance-of-payments grounds. This it could attempt to do by intervening in the foreign exchange market, selling its own currency and buying foreign currencies so that the value of its currency was unnecessarily depreciated and its exports were made unnecessarily cheap in terms of foreign currencies.

Far and away the best method of coping with this set of problems would be for all the national governments concerned to agree (1) that no national authorities would intervene in freely floating foreign exchange markets, but (2) that they would set up a single supranational exchange equalisation fund to carry out such interventions. Such a fund would be provided at its inception with large holdings of the national currencies of the member countries.[1] Its directors would be under instruction to intervene in the foreign exchange markets by selling one particular currency out of its fund in order to purchase another particular currency to hold in its fund with the sole purpose of offsetting what in their judgement were temporary departures from the movements of exchange rates which would serve in the longer run to maintain equalibrium in national balances of payments.

The intelligent radical will attempt to call the authorities of the developed, industrial countries of the free world to their senses. Let them give up trying to form exclusive regional commercial

---

[1] The existing International Monetary Fund could readily be transformed into such an institution.

blocs and promote instead a comprehensive free-trade code to be adopted simultaneously by all the developed countries of the free-enterprise world. Let them give up trying to fix par rates of exchange and fussing about the correct level of international liquidity and concentrate their attentions, domestically, on the control of inflation and, internationally, on the institution of a supranational exchange equalisation fund to operate in a régime of otherwise freely floating national currencies.

IX

The International Setting:
(2) *Controls over Trade and Factor Movements*

In the preceding Chapter we have discussed the steps which might
be taken both by unilateral national action and also by international agreement to integrate the underlying price mechanism of
a country like the United Kingdom into the market mechanisms
of similar developed countries. But just as in our discussion of
domestic economic policy we found that on the foundation of the
price mechanism there must be built a superstructure of governmental interventions (Chapters II to VII), so also in the case of
the international operation of the price mechanism there is need
for a superstructure of controls and interventions. In this Chapter
we turn to an analysis of the nature of these controls over international economic relations.

There are many cases in which there is an obvious need for
direct international controls. The following are three straightforward examples :

(1) We have already referred (pages 114–115 above) to the need
to control whaling on the grounds that, since the whales in the
free oceans belong to no one in particular, no individual competitive whaler will have any incentive to avoid excessive whaling
in order to conserve the stock of whales. But since whaling in any
given ocean will be carried on by whalers from many different
nations, control over the number of whales caught must clearly
take the form of an international control.

(2) There are many internal rivers, lakes, and other waterways
which are shared by a number of different countries. If the
Germans pollute the Rhine, the foul water will flow through the
Netherlands. Clearly some form of joint international control is
indicated.

(3) The noise and atmospheric pollution caused by aircraft on
international flights will affect a number of countries over which
the international flight takes place. Once again there is need for
some international control.

The same sort of case for direct international control may arise
in connection with the planning of economic structures. A good

example of this is the network of transport facilities over a number of contiguous countries. Should a railway link be constructed between two cities which lie in two different, but adjacent nation states? Or would it be more desirable to develop the structure of roads to cope with the traffic concerned?

Another set of decisions, concerning the planning of economic structures, is involved in regional planning by national governments. These decisions also can have far-reaching international implications. An industrial centre requires a large social infrastructure covering the supply of electricity, gas, water, transport facilities, telephone connections, and so on. As a result of this there may well be a cumulative effect in the growth of an industrial region. The existence of some industry and some suitable infrastructure will attract more industry and lead to the development of more infrastructure. A region which happens to make a good start may drain activity away from a region which happens to make a bad start. A national government may thus have a very legitimate interest in influencing (by subsidy, tax, or other controls) the structure of regional development. It is an example on a large scale of a government's interest in the geographical structure of the use of land of the kind to which reference has already been made in Chapter VII (see page 108 above).

But national regional planning of this kind may raise some very obvious international issues. There may be two regions, A and B, both suitable for industrial development of a certain kind. The size of the market for the products concerned may justify the development of one but not of both of these regions. Should region A or region B be encouraged for this further industrial development? If region A is in one national state and region B in another, the conflict of national interest is clear. Should A's products be encouraged to supplant B's, or vice versa? Some form of international decision-making machinery would clearly be desirable.

The provision of public goods may illustrate a case where international decision and control is desirable, even if it is not essential. The outstanding example is national defence. Consider a group of countries (such as the members of the European Economic Community) which have forgotten their old national enmities and are concerned solely with joint defence against possible aggression from outside. In any defence programme there are three distinct questions : (1) Who is to bear the costs? (2) Who is to produce the weapons? and (3) Where are the weapons to be used? In the case of one country such as the United Kingdom it would clearly be ridiculous to argue that for the defence of the

Kentish coast (1) the residents of Kent should be taxed to purchase (2) tanks produced in Kentish factories to be deployed (3) along the Kentish coast. It might be more reasonable to say that (1) the rich citizens of Bournemouth and elsewhere should be taxed to purchase (2) tanks produced in the Midlands for deployment (3) along the Kentish coast.

A combined defence programme by a group of nation states involves the same principles. The most effective defence programme for the European Economic Community as a whole, financed in the most equitable manner, would be one in which : (1) funds were raised by the progressive taxation of all the citizens of all the member countries according to their individual levels of income, consumption, or wealth; (2) these funds were spent on the purchase of weapons from whatever sources of supply could provide them most cheaply throughout the community;[1] and (3) these weapons were deployed in whatever region of the community was considered most effective on military grounds. But the implications of these principles for international economic controls are very far-reaching. In their complete form they would involve nothing less than a supranational budget with a supranational governmental authority for the whole community, endowed with the power of raising the necessary taxes and deciding on the purchase of the military supplies and on their development.

A less dramatic form of public good in the provision of which international action, though not essential, would be beneficial is the organisation and finance of research and development. We have already considered this question in its national aspect (see pages 47–49 above); but the analysis has a clear international application. Research and development involves expenditure on real economic resources of men, scientific equipment, and so on. But the use of any resulting new idea or knowledge of a new technique is a public good – the fact that Mr A uses the idea in his line of business does not mean that the idea is no longer available for Mr B to use in his business also. This characteristic of research and development transcends national frontiers. Successful research

---

[1] The fact that the funds raised by taxation of the citizens of one particular member state of the Community would not be tied to expenditure on military supplies produced in that particular member state is one example of the principle of untied loans and grants discussed above (page 133). Balances of payments would become more sensitive to changes in relative prices in so far as taxes raised in one country could be diverted from the purchase of one country's products to those of another country according to the relative cost of production of the supplies in question.

carried out in French laboratories will produce ideas which Germans and Italians could use without depriving the French of the use of the idea. The case for a joint finance of research and development through a single international budget, the research being located wherever seems best on grounds of cost and scientific ability and the results of the research being at the free disposal of all users, is on all fours with the case for a joint international budget for defence, the defence activities being located wherever seems best on economic and military grounds and the outcome affecting the security of all citizens throughout the community of nations concerned.

The international implications of national interventions and social controls may take forms which are less obvious than those considered so far in this Chapter. Consider the following example of the application to international trade of the problems involved in the correction of divergences between social and private costs and benefits in any one particular line of activity. Suppose that it were considered by the government of a country like the United Kingdom (1) that the use of cars involved certain social costs (such as congestion, noise, pollution of the atmosphere) which should be charged to the user of cars in the community by means of a tax, but (2) that, at the same time, the production of cars in the economy involved certain social benefits (such as the spread of technical engineering know-how throughout the community) which should be encouraged by means of a subsidy to the producers. As a result the government imposes a tax of £100 on every car which is purchased for domestic use, but pays a subsidy of £100 on every car which is produced domestically.

As far as cars are produced at home for use at home the subsidy just offsets the tax. The producer receives £100 from the government to encourage his engineering business, but is charged £100 in tax to discourage him from adding to the congestion on the roads. But the subsidy and tax will have a very significant effect upon foreign trade. The production of cars for export will receive the £100 subsidy without any offsetting tax; the import of foreign cars will be taxed £100 without any offsetting subsidy. If the country has committed itself to a general code of free-trade (as was advocated in the preceding Chapter) it would not be very suitable that it should remain completely free to impose a £100 tax on the import of cars plus a £100 subsidy on the export of cars on the specious grounds of a desirable national control over social costs and benefits.

The example which has just been given is a very crude one,

chosen not so much for its realism as for its simplicity in illustration of the general principle that national social controls may have indirect international implications. There are many more realistic examples of this.

Two countries may adopt different principles for the pricing of the products of the same industry. The nationalised steel industry of country A may charge prices equal to short-run marginal costs, while the free-enterprise industry of country B charges administered prices covering long-run average costs. Or national legislation for the control of monopolies may be less restrictive for certain forms of large-scale monopolistic enterprise in country A than in country B. In both these cases it is very possible that these particular lines of production will be encouraged in country A relatively to production in country B not because such production is in any real sense less costly in A than in B but because the national controls in A differ from those in B.

Clearly the same sort of issue can be raised by differences in tax systems. Suppose that in country A there is a heavy tax on company profits whereas in country B the intelligent radical's advice (discussed on pages 40–47 above) has been adopted to shift from a tax on company profits to a tax levied progressively according to the number of workers employed by the company in question. There would be a tendency for tax reasons for a concentration of small-scale business in country B and of large-scale businesses in country A even though on grounds of basic economic cost there was no real advantage in economic efficiency for industries in which small-scale enterprise was possible to be concentrated in B and industries in which large-scale enterprise was inevitable to be located in A. There is an obvious case for the harmonisation of the principles of taxation as between the various competing countries.

The fundamental implication of these considerations is that it is not possible for the developed industrialised countries to bind themselves to a strict and effective free-trade code (such as that advocated in the preceding Chapter) and at the same time to retain complete freedom of action to intervene in their national economies (by taxes, subsidies, or other means) to encourage or discourage any particular line of consumption or production on social grounds. The logic of the argument points inexorably in the direction of some measure of international or supranational control over these social interventions, in which the whole international community is involved.

Up to this point nothing has been said about the movement of factors of production from one country to another. It has been argued (pages 42–43 above) that an important advantage of the workings of an effective market price mechanism domestically is that it will attract economic resources (both labour and capital) from employment in which the value of their output is low to employments in which the value of their output is high. In principle there is no reason why such movements should not be advantageous even though they may mean movements across national frontiers. If capital resources will earn a real rate of return of only 10 per cent in the production of shirts in Ruritania but can earn 15 per cent in the production of shoes in Arcadia and if there is free trade in shirts and shoes between Ruritania and Arcadia so that the valuation put upon shoes and shirts takes place in a single integrated Ruritanian-Arcadian market, then the value of the combined outputs of the integrated Ruritanian-Arcadian economy will be raised by the movement of capital from the Ruritanian shirt industry to the Arcadian shoe industry. Similarly if the value put by consumers on the product of labour in the Arcadian shoe industry is higher than that put on the product of labour in the Ruritanian shirt industry the free movement of labour from the Ruritanian shirt industry to the Arcadian shoe industry will raise the value of the combined outputs of the two integrated economies. The intelligent radical thus starts with the presupposition that the integration of the commerce of the developed countries into a single free-trade complex should be supplemented with the free movement of factors of production between them.

But there are some special reasons for controls over the international movements of capital and labour which the intelligent radical will recognise.

Consider first the case of the movement of capital from one country to another. This will take the form of the movement of funds from the purchase of assets in, say, the United States to the purchase of assets in, say, France if the rate of return on capital assets is higher in France than in the United States. With the international monetary mechanism discussed in Chapter VIII this transfer would take the following form. The purchase of francs with dollars by those who wished to move capital funds from the United States to France would cause the dollar to depreciate and the franc to appreciate in the foreign exchange markets. The depreciation of the dollar would make American products cheaper in world markets and the appreciation of the franc would make French products more expensive. French imports would rise and French exports would fall, whereas American imports would fall and American exports would increase. Real resources would thus be transferred from the United States to France to correspond with the transfer of monetary capital funds.

It should be noted that the transfer of real capital resources from America to France need not take the form of the transfer of capital goods (machinery etc.) from America to France. The price mechanism may work in the following way : less resources are invested in the production of machinery in America for use in American industry and these resources are attracted into the production of cars for export which has become more profitable because of the depreciation of the dollar; and in France more resources are invested in the production of machinery in France for use in French industry, these resources being attracted from the production of cars in France which are in turn replaced by the cheaper American cars. Moreover, the transfer might well be through third countries; American exports to Germany, for example, might increase because of the decline in the price of American products relatively to German products and, as an offset to this, German exports to France might increase because of the increase in the price of French products relatively to German products.

If the American loan is not tied to any particular products of any particular country, a flexible international price mechanism of the kind outlined in Chapter VIII will help to transmit the real capital resources from the United States to France by the easiest and most efficient routes by suitable adjustments of all the different imports and exports of all the countries concerned in the integrated world market.

Thus normal movements of capital from one developed country to another should present no special balance-of-payments problems if the mechanisms for balance-of-payments adjustments discussed in Chapter VIII are in operation. It is, however, possible that some specially agreed international governmental measures might be desirable to mitigate the balance-of-payments effects of very large and very sudden changes in capital movements. We may take the problems presented by the recent dramatic rise in the price of oil as a possible case in point.

The oil-producing countries suddenly raised very substantially the price charged for their oil exports to the developed industrialised countries. Consumers in these countries had to pay much more for their direct and indirect consumption of oil and the products of oil. If the oil-producing countries do not themselves spend on United Kingdom products their increased receipts of pounds obtained from the United Kingdom consumers of the more expensive imported oil, there will be a net deflation in the demands for United Kingdom products, since United Kingdom consumers have less of their incomes left over to spend on products other than imported oil. If the United Kingdom were adopting the financial policy advocated in Chapter II, the authorities would take financial measures to offset this deflation of demand for United Kingdom products so as to avoid any deflation in the stabilised index of domestic prices or incomes.

If the oil producers invested their excess receipts for the oil sold in the United Kingdom in assets of one kind or another in pounds sterling in the United Kingdom, that for the time being at least would be the end of the story. The United Kingdom would be consuming the same amount of its own products, it would have an increased trade deficit because of the rise in the price of oil imports, but the oil producers would be lending a similar amount to the United Kingdom.

But the story would be different if the oil-producers having acquired a large surplus of pounds sterling from their sales of oil to the United Kingdom wished to invest these sums in dollar securities. There would then be a very large and sudden movement of capital funds from pounds into dollars. It might be quite impossible through the mechanism of exchange-rate variation for the United Kingdom to generate at all quickly the vast trade surplus and for the United States to generate at all quickly the vast trade deficit which would be required to finance this vast movement of capital funds. In the last Chapter (pages 129–132) we have considered the problem of time-lags in the adjustment of trade channels and of the consequential need for private speculative funds or for official exchange equalisation funds to fill temporary gaps in balances of payments. This movement of oil-producers' funds would be an example of this particular problem in a highly magnified form. Its mere size and abruptness calls for special measures by the oil-importing countries to offset the movement of such oil funds by official loans from one national government or monetary authority to another.

Apart from such special balance-of-payments offsets to meet specially large and abrupt movements, there is one other way in which international co-operative action may be desirable to deal with balance-of-payments problems caused by international capital movements. Suppose that there is a threat of domestic inflation in both the United Kingdom and the United States. Suppose that in both countries the authorities, on the principles discussed in Chapter II, have decided to take financial measures to restrict total demand. But suppose that in the United Kingdom these measures take a fiscal form (i.e. increased rates of tax and increased budget surplus), whereas in the United States they take a monetary form (i.e. higher interest rates). The rise in interest rates in the United States might attract large sums of short-term capital from the United Kingdom, thus putting a severe temporary strain on the United Kingdom balance of payments.

If the divergence between interest rates in the United States and the United Kingdom were merely the temporary result of different financial policies for short-run control of domestic inflations or deflations of demand, there is a strong case for their avoidance as far as possible by international co-operation in the use of financial weapons of control. If the United Kingdom were willing to agree to rely rather more on monetary measures and rather less on fiscal measures and the United States were willing to agree to rely rather more on fiscal and rather less on monetary measures, the temporary disequilibrium in balances of payments due to large-scale short-term capital movements might be avoided.[1]

If the developed countries adopted flexible price-mechanism methods of coping with international trade and payments, such as those discused in Chapter VIII, the balance-of-payments problems presented by free international capital movements should not

[1] This argument refers only to temporary divergences in interest rates due to differences in short-term measures for domestic stabilisation purposes. The position is quite different if the divergences are due to differences in long-run structural policies. Thus suppose that interest rates are permanently lower in the United Kingdom because the authorities have decided that there shall be a large permanent budget surplus in order to devote an exceptionally large proportion of the national income to savings. Then a long-run continuous movement of savings from the United Kingdom (where the real rate of return on invested funds is depressed by the high level of savings which need investment outlets) to the United States (where the real rate of return on such savings is maintained at a permanently higher level) may properly be allowed to exercise its long-run structural effect in keeping the pound sufficiently depreciated in terms of dollars to stimulate United Kingdom exports and to restrain American exports so as to enable a real transfer of resources from the United Kingdom to the United States to take place. In these circumstances saved capital is permanently more productive in real terms if it is invested in the United States than if it is invested in the United Kingdom.

prove too difficult to solve. Much more fundamental problems however are presented by divergences in other national control policies which affect the returns to labour and capital in different countries.

Suppose for example that there were much more severe controls in country A than in country B over the maximum prices which might be charged by monopolistic concerns or over the restrictive practices of one kind or another which such concerns might be tempted to adopt. There might result a powerful inducement to move capital funds from country B in order to develop such concerns in country A, even though there was in fact no real social productive advantage in carrying on these activities in A rather than in B. Harmonisation of policies for the control of monopolistic practices in A and in B would clearly be desirable.

Similar problems can arise because tax rates are not harmonised. Suppose that the real rate of return on capital investments is only 10 per cent in A whereas it is 15 per cent in B. The total output of A and B combined would be increased by a movement of capital from A to B. But suppose that there is a rate of tax of only 20 per cent on profits in A, whereas the rate of tax in B is 50 per cent. The post-tax rate of return will be 8 per cent in A but only $7\frac{1}{2}$ per cent in B. Capital resources will be attracted in the perverse direction from B to A.

This perverse movement of capital funds could be avoided if by agreement between the governments of A and B tax rates were imposed according to the residence of the recipients of profits rather than according to the source of the profits. In other words residents in B would be taxed at a rate of 50 per cent on all profits which they received, whether these originated from investments in B or in A; and similarly residents in A would be taxed at a rate of 20 per cent on all profits which they received, whether these profits had their origin in A's or in B's industries. Residents in A and residents in B would both obtain a higher post-tax yield from investments in B's industries than from investments in A's industries, and capital would be tempted to flow in the socially desirable direction.

But now there would be a tax incentive for owners of property to move their residences from B to A in order to be taxed only at 20 per cent instead of 50 per cent. This tax incentive could introduce another kind of distortion. It might be more efficient for people to live and work in B than in A either because of certain environmental differences (e.g. a better climate or less congestion of population in B than in A) or for reasons of productive efficiency. Many property-owners are also workers. For an individual to move from B to A in order to escape taxation on his income from property may involve his moving from a place in which his labour is more productive to a place where it is less productive.

Uneconomic migrations of labour may, of course, be caused much more directly by differences in rates of tax on earned incomes. If a worker can produce an output worth £1,000 in A, but can produce an output worth £1,500 in B, the total combined output of the two countries would be increased by a migration of labour from A to B. But if the rate of tax on earnings were 20 per cent in A and 50 per cent in B, the post-tax rewards would be £800 in A and £750 in B; and there would once again be an incentive for a perverse migration from B to A.

Let us illustrate the inefficiences that might occur in the international economy with free movements of capital and labour but without tax harmonisation by taking an extreme and rather fanciful example. Suppose that in one country there were an extreme philosophy of social welfare involving extremely high and progressive taxes on the incomes and the property of the rich and extremely generous subsidies to the incomes of the poor. Suppose that simultaneously in an adjacent country there were an extreme philosophy of self-help and individual incentives with a minimum of redistributive finance. If there were completely free and very easy mobility of persons and capital funds between these two countries, then the rich, able, enterprising and energetic members of society would move from the 'welfare-state' country to the 'self-help' country, while the poor, feeble, unenterprising, and slack citizens would congregate in the former. The result would be catastrophically inefficient.

The obvious moral is that, if free movements of labour and capital are to be permitted, rates of taxation should be harmonised in the countries concerned. But the international harmonisation of tax rates has very far-reaching implications which we can illustrate most vividly by making the extreme assumption that there has been complete harmonisation of tax rates in all the countries concerned.

Not all countries will be equally well endowed with economic resources. Some will be richer than others. If there is complete harmonisation of tax rates, then with any given progressive structure of taxes on the rich and subsidies to the poor, budget revenues will be exceptionally high in the rich countries and low in the poor countries, whereas budget outgoings will be exceptionally low in the former and high in the latter. The budget surpluses of the rich countries will be needed to finance the budget deficits of the poor countries.

In other words complete tax harmonisation would, of course, mean that all the countries concerned would have to agree on the same fiscal policies for the domestic redistributions of income and wealth, because complete tax harmonisation simply means agreement on the same schedules of taxes and subsidies. Redistributional philosophies and policies could no longer remain matters for independent national choice. But the implication is really even more far-reaching. Something approaching a single supranational budget would be needed whereby the excess tax revenue of the rich countries was used to finance the excess subsidisation of the poor of the less wealthy countries.

Any movement in the direction of a joint supranational budget to cope with tax harmonisation and its redistributive effects would raise the demographic issue to which reference was made in Chapter VII (pages 120–122). As we have seen one reason for a low income per head is a large number of dependent children in the family so that redistributive finance inevitably involves taxing the childless in order to help to support the large families. The international implication of this would be that other things being equal, the countries with restrained fertility would be sub-subsidising the high-fertility population-explosion countries.

Differences in demographic conditions raise an even more obvious issue. With a given total population it is no doubt desirable that labour should move from points of low to points of high productivity, which – provided that taxes and subsidies have been appropriately harmonised – means movement from points of low to points of high income. But suppose that the low income is due to a pressure of numbers on economic resources resulting from the fact that population is growing too rapidly in the low-income country, while the high income is due to the fact that there is no population explosion and for that reason no pressure of numbers on economic resources in the high-income country. Suppose that the demographic relief due to emigration from the population-explosion country will merely remove restraints on the further growth of numbers in that country. There is a clear case for the control of immigration into the high-income country, since migration will in this case ultimately lead to overpopulation in both countries. The free movement of labour may call for the harmonisation of population policies as well as for a harmonisation of tax policies.

These difficulties should not be exaggerated in the case of the developed countries.

In the first place, labour and capital are not perfectly mobile internationally. Migration is costly; and in addition to the actual money costs of movement, language barriers, national sentiment, differences in social customs, ignorance of conditions in other countries, and pure inertia means that there can be appreciable divergences in post-tax returns to labour and capital without these leading to excessive international movements of capital and labour. Complete tax harmonisation is not needed.

Second, all the developed countries are relatively rich; and in so far as there are no extreme differences between rich and poor countries, tax harmonisation can go a considerable way without involving large budget surpluses in rich countries and deficits in poor countries.

Third, birth rates have come down very substantially in the great majority of the developed countries and there are as a result smaller differences in the rates of growth of population in the countries concerned.

But these difficulties are extremely great as between the developed, industrialised countries on the one hand and the less developed unindustrialised countries on the other. There are extreme differences in real income per head between the affluent developed countries and some of the poverty-stricken undeveloped countries. There are also extreme differences between the low birth rates and moderate rates of growth of population in most of the developed countries and the high birth rates and explosions of population in many of the undeveloped countries. Fiscal harmonisation (for example, the payment to every Indian peasant of a social dividend of the kind suggested in Chapter VI for countries like the United Kingdom) would involve huge subsidisation of the governmental budgets of the undeveloped countries out of the budget surpluses of the developed countries. Extensive fiscal harmonisation is out of the question and there is a strong case for some control over migration.

The hideous disparities in real income between rich and poor countries and the terrible threat from the present explosion of world population are probably the two most fundamental economic problems in the world today. In this book, which is directed towards the measures which a country like the United Kingdom should take in order to put its own house in order, it is impossible to embark on any adequate discusion of these wider problems.

The intelligent radical in a developed country like the United Kingdom will certainly recognise their extreme importance and will realise that, as soon as his own house is in order, they will dominate his thoughts. These thoughts will run on the following lines.

As has already been suggested (page 132 above), in any general code for the adoption of free trade principles the developed countries should be prepared to admit imports freely from all sources, including the undeveloped countries, without demanding in return that the undeveloped countries should admit freely the products of the developed countries. The ability of the undeveloped countries, as they industrialise, to sell freely their manufactured products – textiles and light engineering products, for example – throughout the vast markets of the developed countries could be of immense help to them. At the same time they would be free to protect their own infant industries.

But aid is needed as well as trade. While it is at present out of the question to proceed to complete harmonisation of fiscal policies for the redistribution of income as between the developed and the undeveloped countries, there should be a substantial development of financial aid from the rich to the poor countries, based on the following principles.

(1) Such aid should be untied. This would not only be helpful for the adjustment of balances of payments (see page 133 above). It would also greatly increase the effectiveness of such aid from the point of view of the undeveloped countries, since they could more freely purchase the type of goods which they needed most for their development.

(2) The contributions to this flow of aid by the individual developed countries should, by binding international agreement, be related in an equitable and systematic way to their capacities to contribute. For example, each such country might undertake a firm commitment to contribute each year a given percentage of its national income.

(3) The expenditure of such contributions should not be left to the national governments concerned, but should be administered internationally. For this purpose these contributions should be paid into two distinct international funds for the aid of the undeveloped countries.

(4) Payments of aid out of the first fund to the undeveloped countries should be made solely in accordance with the economic needs of the countries concerned. Political considerations should be disregarded. Some systematic economic criterion of need should

be adopted, such as payment in proportion to the extent by which the income per head of the recipient country fell below some agreed standard level.

(5) The second aid fund would be devoted solely to projects for the control and reduction of fertility rates in the countries concerned. Restraint of the present world population explosion must be recognised as a quite exceptional objective of international policy.

In this Chapter we have surveyed very quickly and rather superficially a wide range of considerations which justify measures of control over international payments, trade, and factor movements. We hope that we have not left the intelligent radical in a confused state of mind. But what in the end is he to make of the international setting for the domestic radical policies discussed in Chapters II to VII?

(1) He will enthusiastically support the idea of a general code for the adoption of free trade by the developed countries of the world.

(2) He will insist that in this code the developed countries should bind themselves to admit freely the products of the undeveloped countries without asking for free entry of their own products into the undeveloped countries.

(3) He will support with equal enthusiasm the principle that the developed countries of the world should allow their balances of payments to be adjusted through variations in the exchange rates between their currencies.

(4) He will demand that the financial authorities of the developed countries should surrender to an international exchange equalisation fund the task of offsetting temporary divergences of exchange rates from what is considered to be their equilibrium trends.

(5) He will recognise that the general principles of free payments, trade, and factor movements will have to be subject to particular interventions for the many reasons which have been discussed in this Chapter. In this connection, while he will start with a prejudice in favour of supranational controls, he will realise that Rome was not built in a day. Rough and ready compromises will in many cases be necessary. In some cases (for example, the control of whaling or of the pollution of a common waterway) full-fledged international control is the obvious and necessary answer. Other cases (such as the provision of defence and of research and development) may be at the other end of the spectrum and remain uncontrolled internationally even though

supranational control or intervention could be beneficial. In between are many cases where more or less far-reaching compromise is possible. In particular any general international code for comprehensive free trade by all developed countries would have to contain general prohibitions against various national interventions (such as the indiscriminate subsidisation of industries) qualified by well-defined procedures by means of which national governments could obtain permission on well-defined social grounds to make use of some well-defined types of national interventions with their domestic economies even though these interventions had significant effects upon the channels of international trade.

(6) In this connection the intelligent radical will recognise that the very general and rather loose obligations accepted in a universal free-trade code may very well be supplemented by a tighter set of obligations as between a smaller group of countries. Countries which are geographically close to each other will have more need to control certain activities (such as the construction of a transport network or the control of environmental pollutants); and countries with similar cultural histories and political institutions may find it easier to develop supranational control authorities. In particular the intelligent radical will support the development of the European Economic Community in so far as it takes measures to plan and control jointly such matters as environmental pollution, defence expenditures, research and development, the structure of regional development, continental transport networks, harmonisation of controls over monopoly, harmonisation of the pricing principles for nationalised industries, tax harmonisation, measures for the redistribution of income and wealth, and population policies. He will oppose the European Economic Community in so far as it remains an obstacle to more universal codes for the freeing of trade by all developed countries and for the adjustment of balances of payments through freely fluctuating exchange rates.

(7) The intelligent radical will keenly support a systematic expansion of untied aid by the developed to the undeveloped countries, divorced from political controls and influence, and distributed internationally according to the economic needs of the undeveloped countries and for the special purpose of population control.

These seven principles refer only to international policies; and they can be effectively applied only if the intelligent radical is successful in his advocacy of domestic measures of the kind which we have outlined in Chapters II to VII. His domestic base must first be established by a restoration of the use of the price mechanism combined (i) with fiscal, monetary, and pricing policies designed to preserve full employment without inflation and (ii) with governmental interventions for the redistribution of income and property, for the control of monopolies, for the provision of public goods, for coping with an uncertain future, and for the correction of divergencies between private and social costs and benefits. The intelligent radical has quite a task ahead of him.

But perhaps the design of a structure of economic reforms, which we have attempted to outline in this book, is the easiest part of his task. For success is based on the assumption that in the reform of society citizens can remain calm, can be fair-minded, and can use their reason. But can the intelligent radical tempt his fellow citizens to be calm, fair-minded, and reasonable by explaining to them the nature of the Good Society which he could in that case put within their grasp?

Appendix

The following articles and lectures by the author are listed in the order in which the topics are treated in the main text of the book.

1 THE CONTROL OF INFLATION

Inaugural Lecture delivered at Cambridge, March 1958, published by the Cambridge University Press, 1958.

2 WAGES AND PRICES IN A MIXED ECONOMY

Wincott Memorial Lecture, London, September 1971, published as Occasional Paper No. 35 by the Institute of Economic Affairs, 1971.

3 IS THE NEW INDUSTRIAL STATE INEVITABLE?

Review – Article of Professor J. K. Galbraith's 'The New Industrial State', published in the *Economic Journal*, June 1967.

4 THE INHERITANCE OF INEQUALITIES

Keynes Lecture, British Academy, December 1973, published by Oxford University Press, 1974.

5 EFFICIENCY, EQUALITY, AND THE OWNERSHIP OF PROPERTY

Lectures at the Business School, Stockholm, May 1964, published by George Allen & Unwin, 1964.

6 THE THEORY OF INDICATIVE PLANNING

Lectures at Manchester University, 1970, published by Manchester University Press, 1970.

7 ECONOMIC POLICY AND THE THREAT OF DOOM

Galton Lecture, delivered at the Ninth Annual Symposium of the Eugenics Society, London, 1972, published in *Resources and Popula-*

tion, edited by B. Benjamin, P. R. Cox, and J. Peel, Academic Press, London, 1973.

8 THE THEORY OF ECONOMIC EXTERNALITIES

Lectures given at the Institut Universitaire de Hautes Etudes Internationales, Geneva, 1972, published by A. W. Sijthoff, Leiden, 1973.

9 POPULATION EXPLOSION, THE STANDARD OF LIVING, AND SOCIAL CONFLICT

Presidential Address to the Royal Economic Society, 1966, published in the *Economic Journal*, June 1967.

10 FOUR ARTICLES PUBLISHED IN THE *Three Banks Review*

'The Case for Variable Exchange Rates', September 1955; 'The Future of International Trade and Payments', June 1961; 'The International Monetary Mechanism', September 1964; 'Exchange-Rate Flexibility', June 1966.

11 PROBLEMS OF ECONOMIC UNION

Walgreen Lectures, Chicago, 1952, published by University of Chicago Press and George Allen & Unwin, 1953.

12 THE BALANCE OF PAYMENTS OF A EUROPEAN FREE-TRADE AREA

Presidential Address to Section F of the British Association, Dublin, 1957, published in the *Economic Journal*, September 1957.

13 UK, COMMONWEALTH, AND COMMON MARKET

Hobart Paper No. 17, published by the Institute of Economic Affairs, Third Edition with preface by Professor Harry G. Johnson, 1970.

14 EUROPEAN MONETARY UNION, *and*
15 THE OBJECTIVES OF ECONOMIC UNION

Papers published in Appendix F of 'European Economic Integration and Monetary Unification', a report by a Study Group to the European Commission, Brussels, October 1973.

Index